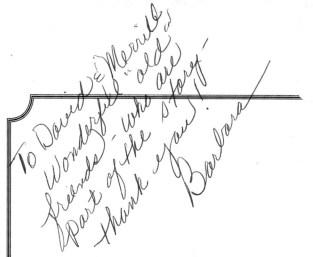

To David & Merrill
Wonderful "old"
friends who are
part of the story!
thank you!
Barbara

Be Your Pet's Best Friend

Choose Wisely, Care Deeply, and Plan Carefully

BARBARA NOVERO LEVY

Cover image by Hallie Murry, a rescue longhair dachsund who happens to
be blind and is owned by Dee Dee Murry. www.hallieart.com

Scrapbook pages by Barbara Novero Levy

Published by AKA-Publishing
AKA-Publishing.com
Columbia, Missouri.

Trade Paperback ISBN: 978-1-936688-63-0

DEDICATION

This book is dedicated to the dozens of friends, professionals, and students who helped me through some very trying and interesting times—I thank you profusely because you kept me from going over the edge on many occasions.

I must also include all my "pet children," especially Sophie and Nessa, who remind me each day that I was chosen to be their keeper.

About the Author

This book is the culmination of thoughts and experiences of longtime pet owner Barbara Novero Levy, who has loved and been owned by fifteen pets in the last 46 years. She inherited her lifelong love of animals from her mother and her paternal grandmother. Growing up, she had three dogs, a cat, a rabbit, two ducks, a chicken, and for a brief two days, even kept a piglet in the basement before it was adopted by a farmer.

Devoting many satisfying years caring for dogs with a variety of ailments has kept Barbara in close contact with her community veterinarian, specialty veterinary clinics, and the College of Veterinary Medicine at the University of Missouri-Columbia. These relationships have made highly specialized care available to her from some of the world's top veterinary clinicians.

Currently retired, Barbara now spends her time writing, and is an active member of the Aging in Place Committee through the Sinclair School of Nursing at the University of Missouri-Columbia. She assists with geriatric pet projects at Tiger Place in conjunction with the Research Center for Human-Animal Interaction (ReCHAI)

She manages home and hearth, but recognizes her role as the Head Keeper of the Cottage, which is "owned" by two Blenheim Cavalier King Charles Spaniels.

Table of Contents

Forever in My Heart

They grab your heart~
Make sure you can do justice
to the relationship and care needs of your pet~
Remember, they give you unconditional love.

— Barbara Novero Levy

INTRODUCTION ·

After thirty plus years in the working world I found myself, like so many others, with an aging self and an aging spouse. In addition to the aging self and the aging spouse, I had aging pets. I spent all those years in business mode in the healthcare industry only to become the caregiver in my own home.

Although I do not profess to be an expert in any specific area of life, being a lifelong caretaker of fifteen pets has given me some depth of experience that I should share.

Like everything in life we all have good intentions and those of us with pet children want to properly care for them, enjoy them and bask in their unconditional love. But along with that we must realize they have needs from the moment we feel them in our hearts until the moment we must part. So you probably know what to do, but where is that helpful list of how to map it out and get it done?

This book is a compilation of topics with guidelines and suggestions to help you formulate ways to do the things you want to do for all those loving years of pet companionship. Hopefully it will help you care for them even if you leave this earth before they do.

Within these pages I reference many different suggestions, but do not endorse any one method of care, specific publication, or product. It is up to each of you to do what you find best for your pet and your family. My goal is to give enough food for thought and reliable references so you can develop your own "things to do" list that will help you to better care for and love your precious pet.

No reference is a complete problem solver, but my hope is that this book will help you get the basics in place by providing guidelines and examples, plus encouragement to keep at it by entertaining you with funny and moving stories that show why it is a good idea to prepare and to care.

Over the years I have had periodic phone calls from friends and work associates asking me all sorts of questions about pets that were ill, pets that needed to be re-homed, etc. One call in particular that comes to mind came from a work associate whose dog had died under a neighbor's porch and she wanted to know what to do next. She had heard me discussing how comforting it was for me to have interred my pet in a local pet cemetery. I shared the number for Memory Park Pet Cemetery with her. She called and they went to her home, picked up her pet, and arranged a simple service to honor her pet. She was most grateful. I did my best for each and every one of my pets.

> So you probably know what to do, but where is that helpful list of how to map it out and get it done?

Pet companions are living, breathing, and feeling organisms. They depend on us to care for them. If you own a pet it is time to put feelings and emotions into your everyday life. In this Internet world keep in mind the "world" of living things does not stop at the back of the screen. Food, water, shelter, and nurturing are all needs that cannot be satisfied via the keyboard and wifi.

So by all means, use your computer to research any pet information you need to learn more about; search for the best deal on a new bed for your buddy or find a coupon for high quality pet food, but always be there with a free hand to touch your pet companion and experience unconditional love for the meager price

> In this Internet world, keep in mind the "world" of living things does not stop at the back of the screen. Food, water, shelter, and nurturing are all needs that cannot be satisfied via the keyboard and wifi.

of some food, some clean water, and bed for the night…all right there is more to it than that sometimes, so read on to find more ways to be the best human companion you can be.

THE BOND AND ANTHROPOMORPHISM

I simply could not write this book without addressing the "spirit" of the subject—the human-animal bond. Keyword search that topic on the Internet and you will be reading until dawn and still not have an end in sight.

There are world-class researchers out there who have been studying this bond for years, but in the last decade this body of research has increased in scope and depth. Having completed an undergraduate course in human-animal interaction with one of these top researchers, and having heard several of her colleagues lecture, I can tell you there is a definite recognition of the bond between us mere mortal humans and the pets we so dearly love. Scientific data points to the benefits this bond has for children, psychologically troubled individuals both young and old, people with dementia, people with physical illness or challenges, people who have had heart attacks, people who live in urban areas, people who live in rural areas…the list goes on and on.

I certainly enjoy reading about these studies and recommend you read a few to acquaint yourself with the body of knowledge that is available. My purpose for introducing you to this body of knowledge and encouraging you to dig deeper into the research is so that you can use the information as the basis for a mature and rational decision on when to get a new pet…or simply to help you appreciate your relationship with your current companion animal(s).

I feel it is important for the reader to understand that I am not launching a campaign designed to influence you to get or not get a pet. I am sharing all my life experiences to help you make the best decision for you, your family, and the animal companion(s) in your life right now.

Being a compartmentalized thinker—I love lists and concise definitions so I will cut to the chase here—I feel so much better owning and being engaged in a relationship with my pets. I feel better on a daily basis, especially if it is not a good day. They often change my mood and my whole sense of well-being. When I am really blue, my animal companions lift me out of the pits of despair and give me reason to move. That in turn makes me feel better physically and mentally. They are my "Rocky Mountain high" without any drugs and hence no side effects.

> **When I am really blue, my animal companions lift me out of the pits of despair and give me reason to move.**

I openly admit that I practice anthropomorphism—there, I said it and I am glad. In plain English, I treat my pets as though they were my children. Since I have no human children, this makes sense to me. Most of my friends and relatives, many of whom enjoy having children and pets in their lives do the same. Only a few peripheral acquaintances view my choice as odd.

I learned of this concept several years ago, but had always been "that way," and had grown up with family who were "that way" with our pets, so I did not give it much thought. Then I took a college course in human-animal interaction and began to see that there are two sides to every issue. The tinge of guilt that prompted me to research this topic more was the feeling that I might be harming my dear little pets. Was I an overbearing stage mom or the ever-hovering helicopter mom? Was I a "mom" at all? I knew they were dogs for heaven's sake. My emotions roller-coastered as I thought of all the poor pets sleeping curled up under a porch somewhere with their only source of water frozen, or out in the heat of summer with no food or shelter, while my "children" slept in a warm bed and had their water bowl washed and refreshed daily.

Thousands of years have passed with the concept of anthropomorphism gaining acceptance, which has led us to think of our pets as having human tendencies. Couple this with evolutionary adaptations and human determination and you get a hot topic. In order to get this all compartmentalized so that I can address this anthropomorphism issue head on, I offer the following thoughts and suggestions on the potential effects of anthropomorphism:

• Companion pets have been bred through centuries to meet human needs and expectations. Breeding to enhance physical characteristics that please the human eye has resulted in negative effects on the health of certain dog breeds. Most notable are those breeds with "smashed faces." These poor canines suffer respiratory and nasal problems that cause them frequent illness and premature death. Why encourage this kind of artificial manipulation of domestic animals? They trust us to do right by them—not breed them to have someone's idea of a perfect-looking head!

• The practice of surgically modifying a pet for "looks" seems a bit over the top. Certain breeds genetically evolved to have floppy ears, and cropping has no positive health effects. In cats, the procedure for declawing has undergone some modifications to make it less painful, but unless the cat is always kept indoors and will never need to climb a tree or protect itself, it is akin to amputating human fingers to stumps.

Current research may not conclusively prove that spaying and neutering our pets will give them longer, healthier lives. The verdict is still out among the researchers. Take these health improvement facts out of this discussion and we are left with a staggering group of verifiable statistics. Hopefully as you review the sobering numbers below you will get a clearer picture of why spaying and neutering are necessary:

> **Between five and nine million companion animals are euthanized each year due to overpopulation in shelters.**

- The largest cause of death among cats and dogs is homelessness due to overpopulation.
- Between five and nine million companion animals are euthanized each year due to overpopulation in shelters.
- Countless pets that do not make it to a shelter are neglected and suffer death because no one cares for them.
- 25% of shelter dogs are purebreds.
- Approximately $2 billion in taxpayer money is spent each year euthanizing unclaimed companion animals.

Here are some salient points to remember when you encounter people with pets or when you are doing your own research:

- Discourage those who do not understand the importance of spay and neuter from breeding a family pet. Also steer clear of those who breed dogs, cats and other pets solely for profit without regard for genetic or health standards. I respect and applaud the conscientious breeders who have taken upon themselves the task of studying genetic factors and other health considerations in breeding to achieve the accepted standards for that breed.

- Learn about your animal companion's personality and needs. Puppy class and/or basic obedience training is almost always helpful. The classes are designed to teach you, the owner of the pet, how to provide consistent commands, behavior modification, and rewards that result in a well-behaved pet and a rewarding owner/pet relationship. Companion animals see humans as the leaders of the pack; they count on us, so don't disappoint. No need to be harsh, but do lead them—they need it.

> **Puppy class and/or basic obedience training is almost always helpful. Companion animals see humans as the leaders of the pack; they count on us, so don't disappoint.**

- Cats and dogs have unique nutritional needs. Selecting the best quality dog or cat food you can afford beats feeding them human food. Always check with your veterinarian and research the foods.

- Spoiling your animal companion can cause separation anxiety. Be a strong but kind leader of the pack and find out what is triggering your pet's anxiety.

- My dogs have hats—yes, hats—I had made that reflect their individual personalities. I do not make them wear the hats even though they stoically sit there for occasional pictures in the hats (they know it pleases me). It causes no harm, so if you dress your dog or buy fancy cat condos I would venture to say that you are practicing anthropomorphism in a perfectly acceptable way—unless the dog eats the hat!

- Without delving into the extensive research on whether companion animals have emotions similar to human emotions, it is widely known and accepted that they are social animals. They like to interact with their human owners. Verbal communication is nice and play is wonderful.

After all this, here is a concise summary of these remarks: Learn what instincts and behavior are normal for your pet and lead from there. Often you will find answers if you watch for signs from the pet, or, if you do not own a pet yet, ask a behaviorist or the owner of a similar pet. When in doubt always ask your veterinarian.

These thoughts are presented to you with the hope that they will inspire you to expand your knowledge base. Then you will become well-equipped with the common sense necessary for your unique situation. Remember, my purpose is not to discourage pet ownership but to help you choose wisely and make your decision the best it can be at the right time for you and your pet.

Costs of Owning an Animal Companion

Everything in life is somehow associated with costs. Owning a pet companion is certainly no exception and has both emotional and financial costs. I deal with the emotional components all through this book, but here I will focus on the financial components.

It is estimated that in 2012, Americans spent $53 billion on our companion animals. Even in a period of sluggish economy, we topped the previous year's spending by almost $3 billion. Obviously that amount triggers a need to more closely examine this facet of pet ownership.

> **Cost must be considered if you want to be a truly responsible pet owner.**

Before we even get into the estimates (and I must stress that these are only estimates), I want to make it very clear that we choose to have animal companions because we love them, so monetary cost should not keep us from owning and enjoying a pet. However, cost must be considered if you want to be a truly responsible pet owner. Let's take a look at the general cost categories and considerations.

Breeder or Pet Store

Costs to purchase a pet can range from $50 to $5,000+ depending on the pedigree, your plans to show the pet, and of course the type and rarity of a particular breed.

The caveat here is to research the breed and the breeder. Learn all you can about the characteristics, temperament, and lifestyle needs of the pet you are considering before you visit with a breeder. Ask your veterinarian pertinent questions and do your own internet and library research beforehand. Do not expect pet store personnel to know all the facts on a particular breed. Above all, do not fall for the "mall effect" of how cute is that doggy in the window without knowing what that breed will be like as an adult animal!

Rescue Group or Shelter Placement

Again it is wise to research or ask friends and your veterinarian about various shelters and rescue groups. Many breed-specific groups offer very educational sites online. Even though they may not offer a totally free adoption, they offer many services to a new pet owner, such as knowledge about the breed, temperament of the pet, and any age or health concerns. Do not be offended by the adoption protocols used by these groups. Remember, their goal is to find the best home for these pets. They offer lots of education and use proven methods to match you with a pet that has the best traits and temperament for your lifestyle. In addition, these groups sometimes offer follow-up placement advice, special rates on training programs, special offers on supplies from retail supporters, and special offers on pet insurance. Also the pets are often spayed or neutered and have up-to-date inoculations.

> **Do not be offended by the adoption protocols used by these groups. Remember, their goal is to find the best home for these pets.**

I have adopted pets in many ways including rescue/shelter groups. Realizing that cost is important, I urge all to consider the value of these groups and the many volunteer hours spent to help the adopted pets. Since many of these groups are charitable entities and depend on donations for their existence, please consider giving them a donation in addition to their adoption fee. If at all possible, try to cover part or all of the costs not included in the adoption fee. These are usually veterinary costs. An additional amount of $50 to $100 is so welcome for these groups. The donation may be tax deductible (check this out with your tax consultant) and will be most appreciated.

> **If money is short you can always ask what they might need in the way of supplies or volunteer help.**

If money is short you can always ask what they might need in the way of supplies or volunteer help. I have donated bags of food, given my time to help with events, and been a contact for a purebred rescue group to identify and help transport pets from shelters. I even served as the secretary for a breed club health research group. But financial help is always good and I often send monetary tributes to these groups as a condolence for a friend's loss of a pet.

Estimated Costs for the Necessities

I have listed the critical categories here since these are the items or services that are necessary for the survival and well-being of your companion animal. There are of course tons of other things that you might want to supply, and there are always life's little surprises that must be dealt with, such as unexpected illness or accidents.

Here is a generic list for your review. The amounts shown are very broad ranges depending on the size of your companion, the number of companions you have, and where you live. Bear in mind, living in the rural Midwest is considerably less expensive than living on either coast or in an urban area.

I strongly recommend that you find current sources of information and costs online and through your vet. Online you will find comprehensive breakdowns of costs by species for small, medium, and large dogs. It is also possible to obtain cost estimations for cats, rabbits, guinea pigs, small mammals, small birds, and fish. The lists below focus primarily on dogs (all sizes) and cats. The broad ranges are shown as estimated monthly costs.

> **I strongly recommend that you find current sources of information online and through your vet.**

Annual Veterinary Care for Healthy Pet

Veterinary care $150-$1000+
(annual check-up/immunizations including annual license)

Monthly Breakdown

Food	$30-$100+
Flea control and heartworm prevention	$40-$75
Litter (cats only)	$10-$50
Toys and treats	$5-$50+
Grooming	$0-$100+
Pet insurance	$7-$75

Estimated One-Time Costs for Pet Needs

Spay/neuter	$75-$400+
Collar and leash	$1-$40+
Microchip	$25-$75+
Litter box	$25-$50
Crate or carrier	$40-$150
Scratching post	$30-$150+

In addition to the above, the items listed below are often not considered until they are needed and then come as a surprise to a new animal owner. Please remember, by the time you discover these needs and their costs, you will already have those paw prints on your heart and will have to find ways to pay for these things. It is important to remember that making a mature decision at the onset is always in the best interests of the owner and the companion animal. We can all find ways to stretch our financial resources, so make sure you consider all the present and future needs so you don't find yourself "stretched to the limit."

> **It is important to remember that making a mature decision at the onset is always in the best interests of the owner and the companion animal.**

Some Additional One-Time and Annual Costs to Consider:

Training classes (highly recommended)	$50-$350
Bed	$10-$200
Fence	$750-$2000+
Bowls	$1-$50
Car restraint	$20-$75
Grooming tools (annually)	$10-$200+
(including shampoo/eye cleanser/dental products)	

Costs That We Rarely Think About Until the Need Arises:

Day care costs	$5.00–$100.00 per day
Boarding costs	$7.00-$100.00 per night
Dental care	$35.00-$250.00+ per cleaning
Professional grooming services	$25.00-$150.00+ per groom
Waste disposal	$40.00-$100.00+ per month

None of the lists include emergency care or treatment of long-term illnesses. Unfortunately life is such that we must prepare for the unexpected. Losing a pet or having to withhold treatment that could save a pets life is truly a heartbreaking event. I urge you to plan ahead for these expenses as difficult as it might be. It is part of being a responsible pet owner.

I strongly recommend investigating pet insurance coverage when you initially adopt a pet. Just as human insurers have exceptions and conditions for insuring a person, similar rules may apply for pets.

There are many companies offering pet coverage, and I highly recommend that you consider obtainingor calculating an estimate using your own research.

Not all pets are eligible for pet insurance, but always research this protection online and weigh the costs of the monthly premium with your best estimate of potential long-term costs. There are many companies offering pet coverage and I highly recommend that you consider obtaining or calculating an estimate using your own research.

You will find that the Internet has a plethora of information about pet insurers, how to assess plans, and how to estimate costs for your dog or cat. There are numerous testimonials from clients that represent a comprehensive list of pet insurance providers. I recommend using one of the many sites to find a company that offers insurance in your state and offers plans appropriate to your pet's needs. The cost of the plan is of course important, but be sure your veterinarian will accept the plan you choose before you enroll.

Money is Not Important to Our Pets

Remember, the thing that costs the least and your pet enjoys the most is your time:

- Take time to talk to them and greet them
- Take time to pet them
- Take time to walk them
- Take time to play. Choose games that do not promote bad habits or undesirable behaviors. (This is as much for you as for them.)
- Take the time to supervise them when they are playing with interactive toys or games until you are sure they will not destroy them or harm themselves
- Take time to nap with them or just watch them nap—there is absolutely nothing more relaxing
- Take time to love them with all your heart because they return it 1,000 times over

Choosing the Best Pet for You/Your Family

Think about your lifestyle and choose a pet that will fit best into that lifestyle. Pets have needs and can only adapt so much—besides, you are the human here and it is your job to make rational choices.

Cat versus dog is the most common dilemma, and since this book does not extend into other choices such as birds, fish, hamsters, ferrets, rabbits, reptiles, etc., I highly recommend you do thorough Internet searches on any of these pets of interest. Although retail pet stores are bound to be knowledgeable, they may not have the full incentive to educate you on all the pros and cons of owning one of these pets.

> **It is a good idea to connect with the representative of a recognized rescue group regarding the type of pet you are considering.**

It is a good idea to connect with the representative of a recognized rescue group regarding the type of pet you are considering. They are experts in all the wrong reasons people choose a particular pet or breed. They can help prevent you from repeating the mistakes of others. It is also beneficial to speak with a local shelter staff member and most definitely with a local veterinarian. Often, veterinary services for non-canine or feline pets are extremely limited due to the special equipment and specific treatments used to care for these pets when they become ill. Also, you should bear in mind that there are city and state ordinances prohibiting certain species. Remember, there are health risks in handling all pets, but some of these less traditional choices can be more risky—a serious consideration when small children are involved.

Never consider wild animals as appropriate pets unless you own a sanctuary for the unfortunate animals that cannot be returned to the wild. Too many of these animals have been abandoned by uneducated persons who adopt them and then turn them out when they discover how unrealistic it is to keep a wild animal in a home or barn. Only persons with specialized training should do this—so do yourself and the animal kingdom a big favor and volunteer at one of the many sanctuaries that struggle to survive each year while trying to protect animals that are unable to return to their natural habitat.

When deciding on the right dog or cat for your family, consider mixed breeds as well as purebreds. Here again you may need to ask for the assistance of a seasoned breed representative from a rescue group, since mixed breeds sometimes inherit two sets of negative traits, especially when it comes to temperament. A shelter representative or breed representative can assist you in evaluating whether or not the pet you are considering has tendencies that are undesirable in your home setting. This is why foster home evaluations are invaluable when considering a placement—these volunteers, their families, and their pets can often help foster pets overcome aggression problems or shyness and can offer you detailed information on a pet's temperament. This information is priceless during the selection process.

If you do decide on a purebred pet, find a licensed breeder who is recognized for sound breeding practices and quality care of their animals. I have dealt with several breeders who practice what I call the "gold standard" in breeding. They screen their prospective puppy owners for compatibility with the breed, and are very helpful with education about the breed in terms of specific care needs and health issues. They place/sell with contracts that protect both the breed and the owner in regard to breeding practices so that genetic diseases can be minimized. In addition, these breeders allow future consultation about the pet and assure that return of the pet would be accepted at any time during the pet's lifetime, regardless of health at the time of the return. So the prices charged by breeders must be viewed with all these factors in mind. Although life offers no guarantees, I have found if you truly want a healthy puppy of a certain breed, finding the right breeder can be an excellent choice. Often, breeders may also have older pets for placement if a puppy is not the right choice for you.

There are many prospective pet owners out there who limit themselves by considering only puppies or kittens. Well of course there is nothing on the face of the earth cuter than a puppy or a kitten. However, please consider the facts—puppies and kittens require much more energy and training than a mature pet. Also, you would be learning about their temperament as you go along instead of choosing the temperament best suited to your lifestyle.

Although it's true that all the cute pictures and expert research available are truly wonderful, the Internet cannot feel the lick on the nose or the quiver of the heart when we relax quietly with our pet.

The following story is an excellent example of how older pets can sometimes be the perfect fit. I feel it has a valuable lesson to share because each of the key people involved demonstrate responsible pet ownership and care.

Our Sophie

Sophie came to us from a dear family who purchased her after careful screening by a very reputable breeder. The breeder sold her with all health certifications on her mom and dad, which is extremely important for this breed. She was sold with a spay/neuter contract, and if for any reason she needed to be re-homed, the breeder had to approve the new owner or would take her back and screen any new owners herself. Sophie was trained in obedience and passed her therapy certification all before her first birthday.

When the family's oldest daughter left to return to college, Sophie was no longer happy on a daily basis with the other family pets. She needed to be an only child or at least have someone around during most of the day. Since her family knew us and knew of our love for the breed and our history as good canine parents, we came to mind as A-list candidates for giving her a new home. Sparing all the details, Sophie came to visit and instantly eased the loneliness I was feeling after the loss of my two elderly pets six months before. Sophie came for a visit and never went back! She stole our hearts as I am sure we all knew was going to happen, and the rest is history.

I am now blessed with a well-socialized, well-bred little girl who came all trained and loved being an only child until she realized she would be alone when we had business outside the house. So, early in our relationship I knew (as moms always do) that my Sophie needed a companion of her own. The next big blessing came during an interview with Sophie's breeder, when I learned that she was going to place Sophie's mother. The next thing I knew, I had made arrangements to pick up Nessa, Sophie's biological mom, in just a few days! Our Nessa was not a puppy but a delightful four-year-old who was so happy to join her daughter and become the canine mom-in-residence. Since they had only been separated for a few months and were both used to other dogs this was perfect—two precious little girls who were beyond the trials of puppy training but still full of life with many healthy happy years ahead of them. I refer to them as my platinum gift of a lifetime.

Although the inspiration for this book started many years ago, I truly believe the presence and snoring background musical accompaniment in my office of these charming little girls has been the final force to get the book done.

I have experienced adoption in all forms: new puppy from a breeder with health clearances and parental traits to compare, re-homing of a three-year-old dog from a breeder, rescue dogs who were traumatized in their birth setting and used for breeding under poor conditions, a re-home with a sudden uprooting from a comfortable home setting. One pet was a true "save" of a dog that was very ill and abandoned at a veterinary college to be euthanized because the owner would not spend the money to do the required surgery.

> **Ask yourself: How much time do I have to devote to a pet? List time segments you can open up in your day for this new family member. Does it add up to a fair deal for the pet? Seek out suggestions and resources on how to make it all work.**

Here is the bottom line—I know not everyone could have taken each of these situations and felt good about the trials and tribulations experienced. But what I know for sure is that the age of the pet was never my ultimate deciding factor, nor did I love the puppies any more than I did the five-year-old who came into my family. My friends have experienced very similar situations and agree with my conclusions.

Since cats and dogs are generally the pets of choice, here is a punch list of things you need to consider prior to adding a pet to your life:

- Will this pet fit into your current lifestyle?
- How much time will you have to care for and nurture this pet?
- Why do you want this pet?
- Do you have the financial resources to own this pet?
- Do you have the proper space to house this pet?
- Will your activity level allow you to share time with this pet?
- What are the daily, weekly, and annual care needs for this pet?
- What level of interest do you have in a 10-15+ year relationship with this pet?
- Are you sure you want to be responsible for another living creature?
- What is your family/other relationship composition?
- What factors listed below do you need to take into consideration?
    - Couple expecting their first child/new baby
    - Working parents with small children
    - Older adults with mobility problems
    - Students with limited space, time and income
    - Family members with allergies
    - Spouses or family who do not agree on pet ownership
    - Other pets in the family
    - Long hours or days away from home

As you determine the impact of the above factors that will apply in your situation, you can move into more specific thoughts about whether a cat or a dog might fit your lifestyle. Seek out suggestions and resources on how to make it all work before you get that new companion. As previously noted, cats and dogs are the primary focus of this book, but I believe this list would be helpful if you are considering any type of pet.

Do the old "this way versus that way" so that you get a real feel for what the options are:

- Cat vs. dog
- Puppy vs. mature dog
- Male vs. female
- Big dog vs. little dog
- Long hair vs. short hair
- Purebred pet vs. mixed breed
- Breeder-purchased purebred vs. purebred rescue pet
- Show quality vs. pet quality

This list could fill the book, but by now I am sure you get the gist of how to really give this subject the consideration it deserves before you make such an important decision. During the years I spent as a part-time rescue representative for Spotsavers Dalmatian Assistance League of St. Louis, I heard many variations on the theme of "why we have to get rid of this pet."

Just a few of the reason's for no longer wanting the pet included:

- My husband just doesn't like the dog (Be sure your spouse is included in the decision-making process.)
- This puppy is hopeless—he goes to the bathroom in the house. (We must all be potty trained—babies and pets alike!)
- I guess he is bored because I am gone all day. (Think ahead if you

work or must leave the pet alone most of the day)

- The kids don't like her any more now that she has grown. (Infants of all species don't stay cute little things forever—they all grow up!)
- I am going on vacation and no one can watch the dog (Consider a boarding facility. Sooner or later you will go on a vacation and the pet will not be able to go along.)
- Cats really do shed a lot. (And you'll be contending with hairballs too.)

I was left drained and often angry at the lack of forethought by adults who got a pet only to give it to a shelter or in some cases just throw the pet away. My heart was broken so many times that I began doing other pet-related support work, but I still feel for all those pets that did nothing wrong and were simply cast away by those they loved.

Not many decisions in life leave us with intense feelings of warmth like having a long loving relationship with a pet. Additionally, nothing is quite as unsettling as having to give up a beloved pet because we or someone near to us made a bad decision when choosing the pet. So remember do your research. Here are a few more resources in addition to those mentioned previously:

- Attend a local dog or cat show to watch, listen, and ask questions— you get to see the best of the breed and pet them too!
- Look into research groups who focus on special needs pets. For example, older dogs make wonderful pets, especially if you are older yourself and just cannot handle a puppy or worry that you might not outlive your pet.
- Get information from a someone who is knowledgeable about the

breed you are interested in, such as a reputable breeder, vet, or rescue group.

- Consider fostering first as sort-of a "test drive."

If you have given all due consideration to deciding on a pet, then you should be proud of yourself. Go put all of your newly gained knowledge to work and go get the pet. Be prepared for the most wonderful time of your life, whether this is a family pet, a show dog, a field trial dog, or your one and only pet companion. Have fun and enjoy life with your pet. After all, the human-animal bond is one of the best emotional bonds we enjoy in life.

> **If you made an impulse purchase or realized you could not keep a pet for any reason and called a rescue, returned it to the breeder, took it to a shelter, or made sure it was adopted by a loving family, then be proud—you did the right thing for the pet and yourself.**

If you made an impulse purchase or realized you could not keep a pet for any reason and called a rescue, returned it to the breeder, took it to a shelter, or made sure it was adopted by a loving family, then be proud— you did the right thing for the pet and yourself. You have mature decision-making skills. If you decide to get a pet later in life you will likely make a more educated choice and enjoy the companionship of your pet even more.

In all good consciousness I must share a sad and cruel fact about uncaring human beings here. You have probably seen newspaper ads or online ads offering a "free dog to good home." Under no circumstances should you place this type of ad. The person who answers this ad might not be the responsible person they present themselves to be. Too often these pets are not cared for or could be sold for research, although this practice is now being regulated in many states. Placing a pet with a rescue group or shelter is always a better option—the odds of the pet being treated humanely are infinitely better than with the "free to good home" option.

If you choose to adopt one of these pets, please ask a shelter or rescue representative how best to do this. This process can involve complicated circumstances such as finding yourself face to face with persons who abused the animal or other family members who do not want to part with the animal. In either of these cases you will need support in deciding what is best for all concerned. You may even need to involve animal protection help or law enforcement.

Hopefully you did all the research about the kind of pet best suited for your lifestyle, all the physical needs and costs associated with owning the pet, the life span of the pet in relation to your own, and of course, daily care requirements and your ability to comply. If this is not

> **Do yourself and the animal kingdom a big favor, and volunteer at one of the many sanctuaries that struggle to survive each year while trying to protect animals that are unable to return to their natural habitat.**

the time to adopt a pet or add another pet to the family, here are a few thoughts on how you might include companion animals in your life in a very meaningful way:

- Volunteer at a shelter or with a rescue group to walk pets during your free time.
- Volunteer with a rescue group to help take pets to a vet or foster over a weekend for the animals that were spayed or neutered that week.
- Foster short-term if you are allowed where you live—sometimes just a few days or a week really helps out the busy rescue representatives.

- Offer to walk pets that are owned by elderly folks if they have had surgery or an ill spouse.
- Help others to manage pet's visits at hospitals or nursing homes on a monthly basis.
- See if anyone in the neighborhood could use a pet walker or pet visitor.

There are many ways to help and enjoy companion animals. I hope this gives you an opportunity to think of more creative ways to enjoy companion animals until you can adopt one of your very own.

> **If you are still unsure of your ability and patience level with a pet of your own, may I suggest one of the many volunteer options that will get you acquainted with behaviors of domestic animals. At the same time you will be helping others!**

We all can and should strive to make a better world for our families, our friends, and our pets. Please use these tips next time you find yourself in a pet selection situation, and if you have children, use this time as an opportunity to teach them valuable life lessons about making informed decisions and respecting other living creatures on this earth.

If you are still not convinced that choosing the right pet requires the utmost care and consideration, here are a few stories that demonstrate the extreme importance of this choice:

What Were They Thinking?

My very first experience with a well-organized and totally volunteer rescue group was with Purebred Dog Rescue of St. Louis. Each breed of dog had a chairperson who was knowledgeable in the breed, so the education about breed characteristics was great. *This particular event occurred right after the release of the movie* 101 Dalmatians, *so this wonderful, exuberant breed was very popular at the time.*

My first experience of interviewing a relinquishing family along with the breed representative was to take place on a Saturday afternoon. However, by Saturday morning the family had called and explained that they had three young children all less than six years of age, they lived in a second floor apartment, and the dog just cost too much to feed and was chewing everything up! They could not wait for our group to come and get the dog that afternoon—it had to go now!

Hmmm…I will spare you my non-professional observations here. For now it is sufficient to say, "What in the world were these people thinking when they bought a large breed dog with high exercise needs while living in a second floor apartment with three young children?"

The family met us on the sidewalk outside a city shelter with the dog in tow—a beautiful male Dalmatian about six months old. They hated to give him up, but the dog was using the house as his bathroom, he was "high strung" and knocked the kids down, he took so much work and was eating like a horse, he was shedding and the kids were tired of their toys being ruined.

I watched the breed representative explain very calmly that the dog was a healthy Dalmatian with typical breed characteristics. We had them sign the appropriate form and assured them he would go to an approved foster home and would then be evaluated for a new home with a yard, a family with older children, etc. They chose for him to go to our organized breed rescue instead of to the city pound. I immediately knew why I had chosen to work with this group. This dog was subsequently adopted into a wonderful home, which may never have happened if this family had surrendered their loving pet to the pound.

The parents just wanted to hand off that leash while the children all looked so sad. I learned how to smile even though my heart was breaking as the Dalmatian watched his family turn and walk away. The Dalmatian went to an approved foster home and was then adopted by a loving and capable family who met the breed rescue criteria.

Two major life lessons I learned that day:

1. As part of a rescue organization, I needed to keep my internal feelings to myself and use every opportunity to EDUCATE people so they could make better decisions when choosing a pet.

2. Children learn responsibility from their parents and need to have a good example set for them when learning how to care for a pet.

Sweet and Innocent Puppy for Sale

As you might imagine by now, not all stories have a happy ending. This circumstance is about a young, well-educated couple with two school-aged children and an infant. The family had had a pet that was trained to stay in the yard and had been a part of the family prior to the children's births. This pet lived a long life and passed away, leaving the older children wanting a pet.

The parents somehow settled on a large breed of working dog after seeing an ad for puppies in the local newspaper. Neither parent had experience with the breed, but the puppies were so cute.

One of the puppies was placed with the family. Of course the children expected the puppy to be as well-trained as the last dog, and when they opened the door the puppy would escape into the unfenced yard. Mom was extremely busy with the newborn. Within a few short weeks the new puppy was killed by a passing motorist on the street near their home.

Once again there are major lessons to be learned:

1.   The educational level of adults does not always guarantee mature decision making.

2.   Breeders sometimes do not care what happens to their puppies. This was an accident waiting to happen given the family's composition and lack of breed familiarity, but the breeder did not seem to care since she sold them the puppy knowing the facts.

The Bedroom Kitty

My friend Mary had been a veterinary assistant for many years and has that special combination of education, experience, and compassion that makes her a gift to all animals and people who know her. Always on the lookout for perfect matches, Mary was visiting one day with the receptionist at her physician's office and consoling this longtime acquaintance on the loss of her cat.

Mary had recently been tapped to assist a friend of mine who was caring for a house full of cats. One of the cats she visited daily was far from social and avoided all the other felines in the house. She had basically relegated herself to the back bedroom. Mary would spend extra time with this cat on her visits and was making very slow but steady progress with some human contact. She was hoping to find a place for this cat, but it was going to have to be a special home.

As the receptionist lamented the loss of her cat that was up in years—nearly fifteen—she commented that she did not want to even think about getting a kitten. She explained that she lived in an apartment and worked all day, and when she returned home she enjoyed seeing her kitty, having a quiet dinner, and then relaxing with her feline companion. They had shared a special bond and she was not at all sure she had the energy or the patience for a kitten.

The wheels began turning and Mary just knew she had to move on this golden opportunity. She spoke to my friend and they agreed that a visit was an excellent idea—so the receptionist was invited to meet the "bedroom" kitty. This kitty was not old, but was certainly mature and was in no mood to join the kitty community where she now lived. How perfect. She would have an apartment to herself all day, her very own human in the evening, and life would be grand.

Well, visit number one with the receptionist and "bedroom" kitty went very well, with the kitty allowing a tiny gentle pet on the first meeting! Everyone left to consider all the possibilities. After one more visit, "bedroom" kitty had a new home and a new life.

Now when Mary goes to the doctor's office she gets regular reports on the wonderful life she created for a lonely kitty and a sad lady who needed that special void in her life filled.

Lessons I learned from this wonderful placement:

1. This is a stellar example of how older pets can be the perfect choice.

2. There are rescue organizations that specialize in placement of older or special needs pets, so the lesson here is to always keep an open heart and remember that an older pet should always be considered for adoption.

Your Best Bet is a Good Vet

From the moment you choose a pet or a pet finds you and you decide to keep it, the first order of business is to develop a relationship with a veterinarian. Plan a meeting with your veterinarian prior to getting a pet in order to discuss breed characteristics, potential health problems, and the cost of treatments available for those problems. You should visit your veterinarian for a complete examination of your pet as soon as possible after adoption/purchase. This will prepare you for future considerations early in the relationship.

> **You should visit your veterinarian for a complete examination of your pet as soon as possible after adoption or purchase.**

In my personal experience, this is one of the most important relationships for both the pet and the pet owner. Those of you who already have a vet will understand, even if your pet is well at this time. The time to establish and nurture this vet/pet/owner relationship is during your annual visit, when the pet is well and the visit is not an emergency.

The best kept secret in the veterinary profession is that they take owners and their pets as a package deal. The pet cannot talk but certainly can communicate via symptoms, and owners can add valuable observations about the pet's behavior and overall scope of the pet's needs. The veterinarian you choose should be well-versed in reading both the pet and the owner and should encourage questions and respect the human-animal bond. Always be up front with them and they will assist you in ensuring that your pet's health and well-being are at the forefront of every visit.

Through all my years and hours of veterinary office visits, both at the community vet and at the specialist's office, I have been continually amazed at the diagnostic skill and evaluation techniques a veterinary professional must have. I have asked them everything, never afraid they might find my inquiry too "stupid" or too unimportant to ask, and never was I made to feel like anything less than a competent and caring individual. I always went home from the visit wondering why many human doctors do not use this same approach.

There were many times this unique veterinary approach saved my pets from the agony of not getting early treatment in a situation. It saved me from wasting money on expensive food that was not really better for my pets and gave me the assurance that no matter how it all turned out, I had done my very best to help them. The guilt is awful beyond description when you find out you could have prevented suffering if you had only asked. For these reasons, I have the utmost respect for the veterinarians, veterinary technicians, and human-animal bond professionals that have touched me and my pets' lives. I encourage you to find a veterinarian that works well with you and your pet as early as possible, and should you need to change veterinarians or need a referral to a specialist, try to hold these future relationships to the same high standard.

Pet ownership is a precious two way street—society believes we own them, but they own us in their way too. The veterinary relationship completes the trilogy of love, ownership, and responsibility. Now go forth and enjoy every moment you can with your pet(s), knowing you have this critical care piece in place.

As you read the following, begin the thought process that will ensure many happy years of the most precious relationship known on earth. Alright, there are other relationships that are precious, yet I can tell you that the human-animal bond often ranks in the top five, and no one need answer what the others are or how they rank. That's the lovely part of life—we can keep some things personal and confidential—the parts that are forever in our hearts. So give this life decision the time it deserves and you will be rewarded with many warm and wonderful years.

What the American Veterinary Medical Association Says About Taking Care of Our Pets:

They begin with the need to commit to the relationship for the life of the pet and the need to avoid impulsive decisions when selecting a pet. They offer guidelines to the care and safety of pets and take us through to the end when we must recognize decline in health and the special care needed at that time. Complete listings of AVMA guidelines can be found on their website.

In November of 2010, the AVMA received a recommendation from their Animal Welfare Committee that led to a revision in the veterinarian's oath. This oath now reads: "Being admitted to the profession of veterinary medicine, I solemnly swear to use my scientific knowledge and skills for the benefit of society through the protection of animal health and welfare and the relief of animal suffering, the conservation of animal resources, the promotion of public health, and the advancement of medical knowledge."

These are very powerful and defining words for a well-respected and admired profession.

Tribute to Dr. Jeff

I am very grateful to have made the acquaintance of some absolutely wonderful veterinarians in my life. I believe I can call many of them friends, and I have my companion canine kids to thank for this wonderful part of my life. I have felt this way for many years, and when I was once asked to write something for a College of Veterinary Medicine marketing piece, I reflected on the recent loss of our nearly fifteen-year-old Cavalier King Charles Spaniel and the excellent long-term care she received. I chose to write a tribute to her, but really ended up writing a tribute to our veterinarian at the time. Here are selected excerpts from the original tribute to our April and Dr. Jeff Coggan, a 1985 graduate of the University of Missouri College of Veterinary Medicine:

Our veterinarian is part of a multi-professional group practice in a suburban area that is booked several days in advance. In the past he had made an occasional house call due to April's shyness and her progressing condition.

Here we were at the worst possible time for an emergency—she had had a severe attack and had passed out. My husband called and this wonderful human being came to our house and knelt by the bedside, where I was reduced to a heaving, crying lump of flesh nearly incapable of speech because I knew the end was near. My husband was hardly able to speak, so Dr. Jeff asked, "Is this her favorite spot?" I nodded yes and he said, "No need to go anywhere else." With my hand on her back, I felt her angel wings sprout and her soul rise toward heaven and the Rainbow Bridge.

My husband and I will always be indebted to Dr. Jeff for recognizing both the human and the canine emotional needs at this time. He and the technician with him recognized the gravity and importance of this moment and they allowed this little girl the peace and dignity she deserved.

Bless this man who truly loves what he does—the good parts, the bad parts, and the painfully human parts.

Bless this man who truly loves what he does—the good parts, the bad parts, and the painfully human parts.

This is a heartfelt example of my feelings toward the numerous veterinarians who have been there for us through the years as we have cared for thirteen pets. Many of our pets were rescued; some had very complex health issues while others enjoyed relatively healthy years. One thing is for sure—without the wonderful veterinarians and some very brilliant residents and veterinary students, my companions would not have enjoyed the great lives they experienced.

Intro to Nanny Manual Pages

No matter how simple or how logical pet sitting may appear, the fact is that the details of caring for your pet must be written down. When these details are needed, the person who is watching your pet may not be able to reach you. You need to keep these instructions in the area of the house where the pets live, so that in case of an emergency the sitter can access the Pet Care Instruction Manual (or whatever you choose to title your guidelines…mine is labeled the Cavalier Nanny Manual). At one point I brought my manual to a specialty veterinarian appointment to ensure I had all the instructions listed. This also gave the veterinarian an immediate medication review.

Except in one or two emergency situations, I was able to review the critical parts of the manual when a pet sitter was being interviewed or was coming for the first time. They found it invaluable. It listed what they needed to know but

> **No matter how simple or how logical pet sitting may appear, the fact is that the details of caring for your pet must be written down. Save everyone the learning curve and write your instructions down.**

also allowed them to meet the pets and know what my expectations were for their care in my absence. They seemed to really appreciate the reference and felt more comfortable in knowing what was expected. Maybe this is the time to remind ourselves that our pets cannot speak. They certainly can communicate in many ways, but will the pet sitter be able to interpret? Save everyone the learning curve and write your instructions down.

The guidelines and formats on the following pages offer a template for the vital information needed to care for your pet if you are not able to do so. Because we all have those very basic routines we do each day, these guidelines should be a good start. Individualization for your pet's specific needs and wants (those things only you know he or she loves, expects, and deserves) can be added as you develop the lists and as the need arises.

As my pets aged, became ill, or trained me on how to best care for them, I added more and more notes to the instructions. Various caregivers came and went—neighbors when my husband was hospitalized for emergency surgery, students from the local university who had jobs as pet sitters (I was fortunate to have both veterinary and nursing students care for my pets). In one long-term situation a beloved relative came and stayed in our home to care for the four pets we had at the time. She found the manual invaluable for making feeding time and outside time more efficient simply by catering to the little idiosyncrasies each of these pets had.

At one point a highly specialized veterinary technician stayed with our pet who suffered from seizures. His medication regime was a sight to behold, and I actually kept a medical chart in a notebook to make sure I was giving medications as ordered and recording his symptoms accurately. Since this was a long-term situation I found documentation was the best memory tool.

Examples of both the routine and the complex are included on the next few pages to serve as guides, so feel free to adapt them for your pet's current situation. Since we have had multiple pets (some with special needs) for many years, I have kept these instructions in a prominent place near the medication and often used separate folders with the pet's picture on the front to make sure the correct pet got the right medication and care.

At the time I was developing the Nanny Manual and caregiver resources, I did not have access to convenient day care programs that could care for my pets. I am happy to report that this long-needed service is being developed in many areas and should be considered by pet owners who work long hours with no one able to care for their pet. It should also be considered by pet owners who want to encourage socialization of their pets. For pet owners using pet day care, I can assure you that having a copy of your pet's Nanny Manual available for day care staff would be invaluable. In addition, being able to grab a copy of the Nanny Manual if you kennel overnight is the best way to ensure your pet's care needs are communicated.

First and foremost, it is important to thoroughly evaluate a kennel and/or daycare provider before entrusting them with the care of your beloved companion. Having someone greet you warmly and tell you your pet is great is a start, but there is much more to consider. All right let's say it, because many of you are thinking it—pet care facility evaluation should be every bit as selective as childcare facility evaluation. So do more than make a phone call; make an appointment to visit the facility without your pet if possible, and then return with your pet to assess their reaction. Get personal references from current clients. Here is a short daycare inspection checklist:

- Cleanliness and set up of facility
- Safety of pets during all activities
- Training of management staff _and_ handlers

- Ratio of dogs to handlers
- How big are playgroups?
- Is there rest time/treats/walk on lead time?
- How readily available is medical help?
- How are new pets introduced?
- Are there special areas for behavioral problems?

In addition to this checklist, here are some special considerations when choosing an overnight kennel:

- How are pets confined during mealtime?
- Are there special diet capabilities and procedures for medication administration/management?
- Do you have night time staffing and fire prevention/extinguishing equipment?

You may want to add to this list as you use your manual and think of more items.

Many of the following pages are designed for use. Feel free to copy these pages and customize them to meet you and your pet's needs. Your best defense against problems developing while you are away or traveling is to be prepared and make sure those you entrust your pets to (either by chance or on purpose) have the information they need to do what they so compassionately do on your behalf.

Sample Pages from a Nanny Manual

We need to talk—

Hello, my name is Barron. Here are a few things I want to tell you so we can be best friends:

When I come up to you and lay my head in your lap I want my ears scratched.

I will let you know when I have to go outside by running to the door. If you don't notice that, I will bark.

I only look like a guard dog. Just talk to me, I like to be social.

I like to be in the room where you are, so just go about your business—I can watch you and keep myself entertained.

I love little kids but do not like it when they run, so I chase them to make them slow down. Tell the kids not to run!

Feed me on time and be sure to give me my pills in cheddar cheese spread. See food and pill directions under feeding instructions.

PET SITTER'S OPERATION MANUAL:

You are at: *(pet's name')s home* _____

Garage # entry code:_____

100 Feline Lane, Pet City, MO

Security company: _____

Primary phone # name/contact: _____

Notes on where we are: _____(Hotel name and phone—ask for me by name)

I am attending the following event/conference:_____

My cell phone number_____

Neighbor next door is: _____

Their phone # _____

Our local veterinarian is:_____ Phone #: _____

Our specialty veterinarian is: _____ Phone #: _____

Emergency after hours vet if different than above vet #'s:

Name_____Phone#_____

Friends/family who can be called to help: _____

Special Instructions (examples):

- *Never close door to basement steps—cat litter box is at bottom of stairs.*
- *Susie is not streetwise—always make sure gates in fenced area are closed and locked before she goes into the yard.*

*Also use this area to list special symptoms a sick pet may experience and when to call the vet or what emergency measures should be taken.

GENERAL INFORMATION ON DAILY ROUTINE:

Breakfast time—7:30 to 8:00 AM
Dinner time—4:00 to 5:00 PM

GRACIE is the smaller of the two girls and has a rust-colored spot on top of her head.

SUSIE is larger and has a freckle near her nose.

Dining with the House Pets:

Put chicken broth/water on their food, just enough to moisten it. This is in the freezer and gets heated in a cup in the microwave for 1 minute or a few seconds more if not thawed. Find chicken on second shelf of freezer in cupcake cups/Ziploc bag.

Gracie's dining room is the navy blue crate.

- She gets 1/3 cup of dry food with chicken and broth and ¾ tsp. of Metamucil sprinkled on top in morning.

- In the afternoon she gets the same food but no Metamucil.

Susie's dining room is the light tan crate.

- She gets just over 1/3 cup of dry food with chicken and broth and ¾ tsp. of Metamucil sprinkled on top in the morning.

- In the afternoon she gets the same food but no Metamucil.

Gracie may not go into her crate to eat until I do this—I make sure the door is wide open, fix her food, step back and let her see her food bowl in my hand, then say, "Crate up Gracie." She trots right into the crate and I put her food in the front left corner and very gently close the door BUT DO NOT LOCK IT. She and Susie both just open their crate doors and come out after they have finished their food.

FOR PET SITTER WHO IS STAYING OVERNIGHT:

Close doors to office off the back entry hall and close door to our bedroom when you leave the house. They can stay in the breakfast room, hallway, and kitchen.

ALSO CLOSE MASTER BEDROOM DOOR AT NIGHT or Sophie will go out and bark at 3:00 AM. If you leave the bedroom door partially open she will go through the house and out her doggy door to do her bathroom chores, however she also may decide to start barking!

There is a glass treat jar on my nightstand—they can have a treat when they go out at night to potty. You have to open the door in the master bedroom to let them go out. The light switch for their area is right by the door.

BE SURE TO TURN OFF HOUSE ALARM SYSTEM BEFORE YOU LET THEM OUT AND THEN TURN IT BACK ON WHEN THEY COME IN.

In Case of a Pee-Pee Accident:

The spray to clean up accidents is under the first sink in the master bathroom (the one you see first). The enzyme cleaner is called "Nature's Miracle" and can be used on rugs or the bare floor. Wipe up urine first and then spray area until saturated and let it dry on its own. This kills the smell and the stain.

Check water bowls in the pet room and our bathroom daily.

MEDICATION GUIDE FOR WINNIE:

Pills are in green/white daily pill holders on top of my nightstand. The digoxin and sildenafil are cut and in a ceramic dish in bottles near the other pills unless they are already put in the pill holder. You usually only need to add them in the morning and evening—they are in the pill holder for 3:00 PM and 10:00 PM.

7:00 AM (in white pill holder on the nightstand)
- PIMOBENDAN 1 ½ tabs (brown scored oblong pill)
- TRAMADOL ½ tab (larger white pill)
- SILDENAFIL ¼ tab (sm. triangular blue pill)
- DIGOXIN ¼ tab (very sm. light yellow pill)
- Two pills can be pressed into one bread bit, so she gets a total of three pieces of bread (with pills).
- Make sure bread is smashed all around pills.

3-3:30 PM (in white pill holder on the nightstand)
- Sildenafil ¼ tab
- Tramadol ½ tab

7:00 PM (in green pill holder)
- Pimobendan 1 ½ tabs (see above for prep)
- Digoxin ¼ tab (see above)

10:00 PM (in green pill holder)
- Sildenafil ¼ tab
- Tramadol ½ tab

WRAP ALL PILLS IN SMALL PIECES OF BREAD TO FORM A LITTLE PIE AROUND THE PILLS. The strawberry cream cheese is in the refrigerator—use a teaspoon or an appetizer spreader to apply it so she can lick any excess cheese off the spoon. SHE WILL LICK THE SPOON OR SPREADER FIRST AND THEN YOU MUST TURN AWAY FROM HER...SHE WILL THEN EAT THE PILL PIES.

Take cheese to bedroom and go to her. Do not deviate from any of these instructions, especially the part about not looking at her. She is a Queen Mum and gets it her way!

PET FIRST AID TIPS

These first aid tips are in no way meant to delay or take the place of taking your pet to your veterinarian or an emergency pet care facility. They are meant to help you assess the situation and seek proper veterinary care as soon as possible.

This section has been included in the book because there are situations where emergency veterinary care is needed and quick assessment and action is necessary. Emergency care may not be readily available at the moment you need it. Your pet may need evaluation of a problem when there is just no one to call at that moment. You need to think calmly and clearly on what to do next.

I strongly recommend you keep this information available and review it with the thought that you may need it someday. You will be at least able to make some level of evaluation to determine what is the safest action for you to take.

Review and discuss these tips with your veterinarian so you will be prepared

Review and discuss these tips with your veterinarian so you will be prepared if you should ever need to put them into action.

if you should ever need to put them into action. This will also give you an opportunity to discuss any special symptoms you may need to watch for if your veterinarian is treating your pet for any illness. This could include side effects of medications or symptoms of the illness that indicate it is getting worse (such as redness of a wound, increased urination, or panting indicating increased pain).

Safety is as important for our pets as it is for humans. As part of your nanny manual it may be helpful to describe the most common examples of pet emergency situations and how to handle them. Listed below are the most frequent emergencies and the first aid steps to get your pet stabilized while you seek professional veterinary help.

A longtime friend who worked in ICU at the University of Missouri Veterinary Medical Teaching Hospital helped me draft what she considered to be the most frequent/important veterinary emergency situations pet owners would encounter. *Please review them and keep a copy handy in your pet care/nanny manual.*

I trust by now you are asking yourself, "OK I did all the right things but my pet is not acting right—what do I do now?"

If you see any of these signs or behaviors, please contact your veterinarian immediately:

- Lack of appetite
- Weight loss
- Collapse
- Persistent coughing
- Dilated pupils in the eyes
- Lethargy (not as active) or weakness
- Blue or pale colored gums
- Restlessness and panting
- Abnormal heart rate

- Pain
- Increased thirst
- Increased urination

Here is more specific information:

Bleeding

Arterial bleeding is life threatening and recognized by bright red blood which bleeds in spurts. It may be difficult to stop and requires that you get the animal to the vet immediately. For any kind of bleeding, place a clean cloth or sterile gauze over the area and apply direct pressure for at least five to seven minutes to stop the bleeding. Do not apply a tourniquet unless absolutely necessary. ***Get your pet to the vet immediately!***

Flesh Wound

If wound is not bleeding it's best not to try to remove debris—this could damage the tissue. Cleanse wound with warm water and cover with a clean towel or gauze pad depending on the size of the wound. Check wound for bleeding or redness. See your veterinarian if the wound does not heal quickly or needs debris removed.

These are less severe wounds that one would consider Band-Aid wounds on a toddler. However, pets have the same needs for assessment and care as humans when they injure themselves. Please review the following general definitions of types of flesh wounds to insure you do not delay necessary treatment for your pet.

The general definition of a flesh wound is a wound that breaks the skin but does not damage bones or vital organs.

Here are some more specific wound definitions to help with your wound assessment:

- An abrasion usually appears on the skin as lines of scraped skin with small spots of bleeding.
- A contusion does not break the skin and is usually called a bruise but can be bleeding under the skin or internally.
- A cut may have little bleeding or may bleed profusely depending upon the depth of the cut and how jagged the edges of the cut are.

In these instances you may follow the treatment suggestion above but if there is any doubt or any other health issue with your pet you should seek advice from your veterinarian as soon as possible to avoid complications due to delayed treatment.

The wounds described below are always considered more serious and require the immediate attention of your veterinarian or an emergency clinic.

You will find pertinent notes in this section on transporting your injured pet.

- A laceration may have little bleeding or may bleed profusely depending on the amount of tissue damage (which is greater than a cut), and usually has ragged edges that do not line up, resulting in a jagged wound.
- A puncture wound will be greater in length/depth and may not bleed as much on the outside, but has more damage on the inside and could be bleeding deep inside the wound.

- An avulsion has heavy rapid bleeding and a noticeable absence of tissue/skin (like a piece of ear missing).
- A crush wound may have irregular margins, but is deeper. This type of injury to the muscle and bone may be noted after an auto accident.
- A missile wound may have both an entry and an exit wound (like a bullet wound) and bleeding can be profuse.

Cover the wound with a clean cloth or bandage to protect the wound and control bleeding. Then seek immediate veterinary treatment.

Unconsciousness

- If due to drowning—clear the lungs by lifting the pet's hindquarters high over its head and squeezing the chest firmly until fluid stops draining out of the mouth.
- If due to electrical shock—DO NOT touch pet until source of electricity is off or animal is no longer in contact with electrical source.
- If due to airway obstruction—sweep the mouth and throat to dislodge and remove the object. See the section on choking.
- If pet is not breathing and has no pulse start CPR.

Vomiting

If a pet vomits and there are no unusual looking particles in the vomit plus the pet acts like they are feeling well, this one-time occurrence should be noted and you should be alert for more vomiting. Vomiting is the forceful expulsion of food or other stomach contents that comes out the mouth.

If a dog or cat vomits more than once or generally appears sick along with the vomiting episode it is time to call the veterinarian. Vomiting may be a symptom of many different illnesses, so the sooner the cause is determined, the better for the pet and for you.

The following symptoms should be reported to your veterinarian immediately if:

- Pet has eaten something toxic or poisonous (see section on poisons and toxins)
- Blood in the pet's vomit
- Pet acts like they want to vomit but nothing comes up or out of the mouth
- Pet appears bloated or has a swollen abdomen
- Pet has a fever (take temperature if possible)
- Pet is depressed/not feeling good
- Pet has pale gums or yellow coloration to gums
- Pet appears in pain (cannot get comfortable or is panting heavily)
- Pet has diarrhea

If pet is still a puppy or a kitten and has not yet had all of its vaccinations—get the pet to the vet!

Be prepared to tell the veterinarian:
- When the vomiting started
- How many times the pet has vomited
- What the vomit looks like (be sure to save a sample in a clean plastic storage bag)
- Any other signs of discomfort with the pet

DO NOT GIVE THE PET ANY MEDICATIONS (INCLUDING OVER-THE-COUNTER DRUGS) OR ANY FOOD OR WATER UNTIL YOU HAVE BEEN ADVISED TO DO SO BY YOUR VETERINARIAN OR EMERGENCY PERSONNEL.

Choking

Foreign objects such as needles, bones, food, or plant material lodged in the throat or the esophagus (lower throat) are common causes of choking. An allergic reaction to a medication, poison, or bee sting can also cause choking.

Gently pull the tongue forward and inspect the mouth area and throat. If you can see an obstruction, hold the mouth open and try to remove it with your fingers or with small pliers, but do so as gently as possible and do not push the object farther down the throat. Be calm and do your best, and get to the veterinarian as soon as possible.

Bee or Wasp Sting

Since bee stings are acidic, apply a paste of baking soda and water. However, wasp stings are alkaline, so neutralize them by applying vinegar or lemon juice. Then apply a cold pack—a few ice cubes in a plastic bag or a frozen bag of vegetables will work just fine. Also apply calamine lotion or antihistamine cream to the area.

If the pet has severe swelling or is having difficulty breathing, get to the veterinarian immediately.

Heat Stroke

The most common causes of heat stroke in pets are:

1. Exposure to excessive heat and/or lack of shade
2. Overexertion in hot weather

Some pets can suffer heat stroke even in mildly warm temperatures depending on their fur coat and their medical condition. Short nose dogs are especially susceptible. Stress can speed up a stroke and make it worse.

> **Some pets can suffer heat stroke even in mildly warm temperatures depending on their fur coat and their medical condition.**

Get the pet to a cool or shaded area. Bathe it in tepid to cool water, but take care not to cool the animal all the way down to its normal body temperature, as its temperature could continue to drop to a dangerously low level (hypothermia). DO NOT USE COLD WATER AS IT MAY SHOCK THE ANIMAL. It is important to get the pet to a veterinarian ASAP, even if its body temperature returns to normal, because there may be damage to kidneys or other organs, making it necessary to further treat the pet. One common example of heat stroke treatment is to administer intravenous fluids.

- Never leave a pet in closed car when you will not be there to observe them or check on them frequently, especially in warm weather.
- If you notice a vehicle with a pet in distress or in danger of harming

themselves or others, immediately try to locate the owner of the vehicle. If no one is around or comes forward in a few minutes, contact the local police and/or animal control immediately.

- Give the law enforcement officer and the animal control officer an accurate evaluation of the situation.
- If you are not familiar with the Good Samaritan laws and/or the animal welfare laws in the area, be sure to ask the officer what you should do until they arrive (acting on your own may not be within the law). Depending upon the circumstances, know what you can and cannot do until they arrive.

Limping

Inspect the limb that appears to be affected, but do so gently. Look for swelling or injuries such as cuts or objects stuck in a paw. Touch or gently squeeze the area to check for pain or a feeling of heat that might indicate infection. If you suspect a fracture, stabilize it by immobilizing the limb immediately, and prepare to safely transport the pet to a veterinarian (see notes on safe transport guidelines). If there are open wounds at the fracture site, be sure to cover them with a clean towel or bandages before transport.

Expelling Foreign Matter from Rectum

Foreign matter which is not stool sometimes appears at the rectal area. If the stool is bloody, the amount of blood and the general condition of the pet may give clues on how urgent the situation is. Contact your veterinarian or emergency clinic for further instructions. If there is material protruding from the rectum and the pet is struggling to expel it, do not pull on the object and do not push on the pet's stomach to assist with the process—you could do more damage to the rectum and the intestines. Proceed to the veterinarian or emergency clinic immediately.

Handling and Transporting Pets in Distress

Since getting to the veterinary office or emergency clinic in the heat of the moment is a very stressful situation, here are some handling and transporting tips that can assist you in making it less cumbersome.

Never assume an injured pet will not bite, scratch, or resist as you move them for transfer to the veterinarian.

> **Refrain from hugging the pet or putting your face near its head.**

Refrain from hugging the pet or putting your face near its head. This is not the time. Use a calm voice to reassure the pet.

Do your best to perform a quick but focused examination of the injury. Stay calm and work slowly and gently. Stop if the pet becomes agitated or you see an immediate need to transport.

Before any transport, try your best to stabilize the injury (stop the bleeding, stabilize a broken limb, check for objects in mouth or throat if the pet is choking). Impromptu splints can be made from rolled magazines or newspapers wrapped with cotton padding and attached to the limb with gauze. Make sure the splint immobilizes the affected area as well as the joints above and below the injury.

- Muzzle dogs if necessary with gauze, a soft towel strip, or stockings.
- Use crates whenever possible.
- Wrap cats or other small animals in a towel so that all feet and legs are held close to the body by the wrap.

- Do not attempt to lift or drag a large injured animal. Improvise a stretcher using a board from your garage, a large throw rug, or a child's plastic sled.

Assessment Hints for the Pet Owner

It is important to know how to properly check your pet's vital signs. This information is especially useful when placing an emergency call to your veterinarian.

Temperature:

Dogs and cats—101°F to 102.5°F is normal
Temperatures below 100°F or above 103°F are abnormal

Use rectal instead of oral thermometers for pets. The newer human digital thermometers are best.

Heart Rate:

- Dogs—70 to 160 beats per minute is the normal range
- Cats—160 to 200 beats per minute is the normal range

Check the heart rate by placing your hand over the pet's chest area, or if you have a stethoscope in the house, place it on the pet's chest and count the heartbeats for 15 seconds. Multiply this number by 4 to get the number of beats per minute.

Respiratory Rates:

- Dogs—10 to 30 breaths per minute (This could be slower for large dogs, or faster for small dogs—count and check with your vet.)
- Cats—20 to 30 breaths per minute

Check respirations by observing the pet's flank raising and lowering (that is one respiration count) or hold a wet finger in front of the nostril and count each time air is expelled. If the animal is breathing through its mouth, count the number of times the chest rises and falls. Count the respiration rate for fifteen seconds and then multiply by four to get the number of respirations per minute.

If possible, it is best to take vital signs when the pet is in a resting state. But in an emergency, this information is very important and must be taken even if the pet is not at rest at that moment. If respirations are labored or pet is choking, always sweep the pet's mouth and throat area for foreign objects that might be preventing air from being inhaled.

Items to Keep in Your Pet's First Aid Kit

- Gauze pads and rolls, rolled cotton, and veterinary self-adhesive elastic wrap
- Rectal thermometer
- Tweezers and small needle-nose pliers
- Antibiotic cream and antiseptic solution
- Calamine lotion and petroleum jelly
- Blunt end scissors to cut bandages or trim pet hair away from a wound
- Eyedropper

Somewhere in a special spot keep old blankets, towels, small pillows, old tube socks, and old baby socks to slip over injured paws. Also, keep your transport units in a place that is easy to get to, and keep that old short bookshelf or flat board in the garage in case you need to improvise a stretcher for an injured pet.

Pets and Pain

Often our pets do not show pain because they do not want to seem vulnerable; this instinctive behavior has been carried through the centuries from when they originally lived in the wild. In modern veterinary medicine, it is recognized that when pain is controlled, a pet is definitely able to heal faster.

These behaviors could mean that your pet is in pain:

- Hiding or being more withdrawn than usual
- Loss of appetite
- Rapid breathing or prolonged panting
- Increased heart rate
- Unusual agitation
- Refusal to lie down or sleep
- Aggressive behavior
- Barking, hissing, biting, or running away if you try to touch them
- Slowed movement or limping

Always observe these signs, and if they persist for any length of time with no apparent reason, consult a veterinarian. Waiting to do so could cause your pet undue suffering—the sooner treatment is received, the less the chance of more serious complications.

Some Common Reasons for Pain Are:

- Injury
- Ingestion of poisons
- Urinary tract infections/diseases
- GI tract disturbances
- Infections of the eyes, ears, or skin
- Diseases of the back or spine
- Cancer
- Arthritis (especially in larger, older dogs)

**Fill in emergency numbers below and tab this page for easy reference:
(You will find another placement for vital emergency info—use both!)**

Local Vet Name:_____

Local Vet Phone:_____

HOTLINE:_____

HOTLINE:_____

Local Emergency Clinic Name:_____

Local Emergency Clinic Phone:_____

POISONS AND TOXINS

"Did your dog or cat just eat something poisonous? Call your veterinarian or Pet Poison Helpline immediately. The sooner a dog poisoning or cat poisoning is diagnosed, the easier, less expensive, and safer it is to treat your pet."
~Quote from the Pet Poison Helpline, Animal Poison Control Center

The very best place to begin presentation of this information is to suggest ways to PREVENT an emergency if at all possible.

I was somewhat astounded to learn that just two of the nationally recognized Pet Poison Helplines answer thousands of calls per month, assisting pet owners whose pets have ingested a poison or have been exposed to a harmful toxin. Just estimating the additional calls to local veterinarians boggles the mind.

Here are the top ten pet toxins reported in 2012:

1. Prescription human medications (top of the list for the last five years)
2. Insecticides
3. Over-the-counter medications
4. Veterinary products and medications
5. Household products

6. People food
7. Chocolate
8. Plants
9. Rodenticides (mice and rat poison)
10. Lawn and garden products

Each of these items must be handled properly or you are putting your pet at risk and setting the stage for an emergency that is not only heartbreaking and expensive, it can sometimes be fatal. Always err on the side of caution—keep medication out of reach and prevent it from dropping on the floor. Read the labels on bottles of insecticides, poisons, and household products. Just plain stop feeding people food—keep pet treats close at hand if you really have to give them food. Hide the chocolate—that's a good idea anyway! Weigh your love of houseplants against the love and well-being of your pet, then take the necessary precautions. Store pesticides in a locked area away from pets. Keep pets away from commercial spraying/lawn areas after applications of spray—they won't spray your pet but the pet will lick their feet after they walk through the treated areas. Read labels and choose the safest products.

Avoid feeding your pets these people foods:

- Chocolate, coffee, and caffeine
- Alcohol
- Avocados
- Macadamia nuts
- Grapes and raisins
- Yeast dough
- Raw or undercooked meat

- Raw or cooked bones that can splinter (chicken bones in particular)
- Raw eggs
- Xylitol found in gums, sweeteners in drinks, and baked goods
- Onions, garlic, and chives
- Milk and milk products
- Salt

The second best action is to BE PREPARED if an emergency poisoning/exposure does takes place or is suspected.

Of course, life happens and I have been faced with all sorts of situations just as you have. What I needed at those moments was the knowledge to assess things and get going to the next step as quickly as possible.

No one could have prepared me for the day my sweet and frisky puppy—Kay Kay the wild child—just jumped up and stole my arthritis medication right out of my fingers as it was on its way to my mouth. It all happened so fast and I knew this was not a good thing. After all we hear on television commercials—lengthy explanations listing all the negative side effects for humans—my first thought was "What in the world will it do to this little puppy?"

At that moment the last thing I wanted to do was run to my computer and start a web search. We all know that websites selling products do not allow easy access to information regarding accidental ingestion of their product. Human poison control centers rarely employ veterinary professionals, and our pets do not react to medications or other ingested objects in the same way as humans.

Needless to say, to this day no one in my house takes medications unless they are in complete control of the pill and we know where the pets are.

A dear friend reminded me about the time her father-in-law visited on Easter and stowed a surprise Easter basket on the floor unbeknownst to them, only to find their Irish Setter had eaten the chocolate bunny before Dad took the basket out of hiding to give to them.

Fortunately our community veterinarian's office was open and could help us in both of these scenarios. This was the quickest and easiest solution, but it is not always possible depending on the time of day and the specifics of the circumstance. There are so many variables; often more expertise is needed and needed post haste to prevent complications.

If your local veterinarian is not available, other alternatives are:

- Call the nearest emergency 24-hour clinic if one is available in your area.

- Call a veterinary teaching hospital if you have one in your state and ask if they have 24-hour coverage and poison control assistance.

- Research these numbers and hours of service and list them on the information page in your phone directory and your nanny manual. Then this information will be there if you should ever need it.

Here are the names and numbers of nationally recognized resources that can guide you if you should find yourself and your pet in need of help and all local resources are not available. This information is current at the time of this publication, and it is important to check periodically that they haven't changed.

The ASPCA Animal Poison Control Center (APCC) and the Pet Poison Helpline have 24/7 coverage by specialty board-certified veterinarians to address your concerns if you suspect your pet has eaten something poisonous or has been exposed to a toxin.

Both of these resources are top-notch and have saved thousands of pets. Both must charge a fee for these highly skilled services, but obviously saving your pet is well worth getting the best help in the shortest time frame. In some instances there is no cost if the product involved is covered by the manufacturer through the Animal Product Safety Service division of the APCC.

> **ASPCA-APCC Hotline**
> **1-888-426-4435 Fee: $65.00**
>
> **Pet Poison Helpline**
> **1-800-213-6680 Fee: $25.00**

Here are the numbers and fee (at the time of this publication):

- ASPCA-APCC Hotline 1-888-426-4435 Fee: $65

- Pet Poison Helpline 1-800-213-6680 Fee: $25 (This fee includes **unlimited** follow-up!)

Tab this page for easy reference and include an additional copy in your phone book, cell phone, and Nanny Manual.

In the suggested reading section in the back of this book, additional information and website references for these resources are included. Additional references to assist with more intensive research in less dire situations are also included for your review. This includes the numbers of pet poison help sites and dog food recall sites.

Fill in emergency numbers below and tab this page for easy reference:

Local Vet Name:_____

Local Vet Phone:_____

HOTLINE:_____

HOTLINE:_____

Local Emergency Clinic Name:_____

Local Emergency Clinic Phone:_____

Internet searches on this subject offer so much information to the general public that we tend to be overwhelmed with all the complex information. It then becomes so cumbersome when an emergency occurs, one might panic and run the other way. The second dilemma with an Internet search is that we usually do not have the background or the time to evaluate the credibility of the information, since there are many biases and opinions to consider with this topic.

During my research I found abundant sites and I was able to discuss this topic with an internationally recognized veterinary toxicologist. As I have mentioned in other areas of the book, living in a college town with a top veterinary college offers resources that often boggle my mind. He was able to guide me to recognized resources and help me present them to you in what I hope is a useful and efficient manner.

My goal then focused on offering a clear and easy way to present the information most helpful in making the best assessment and getting the proper care for your beloved pet as quickly as possible. I was astounded at the number of toxins that must be considered. Research the ASPCA website to find a comprehensive listing of poisons. The list can be accessed alphabetically or in its entirety and printed for future reference. This would be another great addition to your Nanny Manual.

Last but not least are the important steps on what to do if you suspect your pet has been poisoned.

ASSESS THE SITUATION—DON'T PANIC.

- Call the veterinary support that is the closest and available (have all the telephone numbers listed according to availability)
- Be ready with information about your pet
- The type of pet (dog, cat, snake, etc.)
- The symptoms the pet is having
- Vomiting, passing blood
- Information about what the pet ate or was exposed to
- Have the container or particles with the packaging and manufacturer's label information handy

In addition, when preparing to transport your poisoned pet:

- Place samples of vomit or stool in plastic bags with closures. Take what you can find or identify of the toxin ingested (medication bottle or sample of the medication, the poison container, the bottle of chemical the pet drank, any pieces of the item the pet chewed and ate) along to the veterinary treatment facility.

- If pet food contamination is a concern, take the remaining pet food in the bag or can with you to the vet.*

- Be sure to talk with a veterinary professional before you induce vomiting or use any liquids to flush away toxins, since this may cause an adverse reaction.

* It is always prudent to do pet food recall research just in case you missed a news release regarding a recent recall of your brand of pet food. The first line of research should be the pet food manufacturer. If you are unable contact your pet food manufacturer, use your Internet search engine and enter: "FDA pet food recalls" and "AVMA pet food recalls." Several sites list all recalls and give information about the reason for the recall.

To sum up this important topic, I offer the age-old advice: prevention is the best medicine. Keeping our pets confined to safe areas or on a leash along with verbal control to call them away from danger is by far the best practice. Keeping cats indoors and pet proofing your house to prevent accessibility to medications, plants, kid toys, etc. is just good practice. Crate training is a useful tool to deter pets from nosing around in all those fateful household items that entice them.

Making sure your pets are properly contained is a very important factor in preventing injuries. Here are some tips to help you avert escape attempts:

- Never open a door until you know where your pet is, and be sure to look right behind you—they do fake you out to dash out the door. This rule applies to all adults, children, and guests who can operate a doorknob.
- Storm doors and half screen doors are wonderful second defense barriers that allow you to open a door if you own an escape artist.
- Fences must be four-sided or attached to houses or other structures to keep pets contained. There is no such thing as a secure fenced area that has fencing on less than four sides or areas that allow digging under the fence.
- Gates must be closed and latched or they are useless.
- When walking your pet, keep it on a leash.

Be aware of your pet's status. Always watch for signs of illness or changes in behavior. Be sure to seek veterinary attention immediately if you suspect something is not right.

These are simply good pet and people practices. Pet toxin and poison awareness can be a great opportunity to teach children about avoiding ingestion of these same "bad things" and helps them learn to identify and reduce exposure to harmful things in their environment.

SAFETY TIPS WHEN TRAVELING WITH PETS

Always secure your pet in a crate if you are traveling long distances. For around town trips I secure my pets in the back seat using safety vests that attach to the seat belts, but during long road trips I use pet carriers for the safety of the animals. I always have identifying information on each crate. You can attach a luggage tag to the crate handle or even just tape this information to the crate. Make sure you include a number to call or direct instructions on where the pet should be taken in case of an emergency. This is just one more reason to have your pets microchipped, since this will be the best way for emergency personnel to get pertinent information should the pet need care or need to be identified. GPS devices are now becoming more available, but remember, these can be easily removed or lost. For that "runner" or fence escape artist these are good ways to locate your pet within your local area, but when traveling many miles from home, services may not be available.

> **Always check ahead to make sure your overnight destination is pet friendly.**

Other Thoughts About Traveling with Pets:

- Take an ample supply of food and water. Just like humans, our pets may not tolerate an unfamiliar water supply without GI disturbances.
- Prepare for climate changes with extra bedding if necessary.
- Always check ahead to make sure your overnight destination is pet friendly, even if you are staying with friends or family. Do not

assume that if they have a pet they will welcome yours, especially if the pets have never met before.

- Remember, new surroundings are not pet-proofed like your home is. Check for any chemicals, escape routes, or doors/gates that are not pet proof.
- If you are traveling a long distance or will be in remote areas, it would be advisable to take an abbreviated health history and immunization record from your local vet along. Store it in a safe place or on one of your electronic devices.
- Never allow a pet to travel in the open bed of a truck unless contained in an anchored crate or harnessed in an approved device anchored to the truck bed.

At the end of this topic is a sample consent form that gives permission to treat our pets in an emergency situation. I have submitted copies to our veterinary sources in both our primary home area and our vacation home area. This way if we were involved in an accident while traveling from one house to another, the tags on the crates would give the contact information for each veterinarian. All the emergency personnel would have to do is decide which place was closer and transport the pets in their crates. Each veterinarian would know what to do and if an emergency vet had to treat the animals, they would have a contact that knew each of the dogs and could assist with the pets' history.

Sample Travel Documents for Pets

Feel free to personalize the form on the following page if you plan to take your pet on vacation. Keep a copy in your glove box and one in your purse or wallet. Always leave one with your local veterinarian so he can give important clinical information and let your consent to treat your pet be known.

SPECIAL NOTE: WHEN TRAVELING WITH YOUR PET, BE SURE YOU ATTACH A SMALL LUGGAGE TAG OR TAPE TAG TO THE PETS COLLAR WITH YOUR CELL NUMBER AND/OR THE NUMBER OF WHERE YOU ARE STAYING IN THAT AREA.   IF YOUR PET IS LOST WHILE YOU ARE TRAVELING, VACATIONING, OR MOVING, AND SOMEONE CALLS YOUR HOME NUMBER OR YOUR LOCAL VET (WHICH IS USUALLY WHAT IS LISTED ON THE COLLAR), YOU WILL NOT BE HOME AND ANY LOCAL CONTACTS LISTED WILL NOT KNOW YOUR CURRENT LOCATION.

To: Clark Animal Hospital (or whom it may concern)

Subject: Levy Pets (list pet and brief description)

During our frequent travel with our four pets, we want to ensure their care if we have a road incident and are unable to transport them to a place of safety or communicate our wishes.

Each crate in our car is labeled with the animal's picture ID. On the reverse side of the tag are instructions to transport the dog to the nearest point:

If found nearer to St. Louis—take to:
Clark Animal Hospital
100 Labrador Lane
St. Louis, MO
314-555-5555

If found nearer to Columbia, MO—take to:
 Veterinary Teaching Hospital
200 Puppy and Kitty Court
Columbia, MO
573-111-1111

This form is intended to give permission to treat our pets' immediate or ongoing medical needs until we are able to communicate. Please make this information readily available in our pets' medical records.

_____   _____
Owner's signature   Owner's signature

Nobody Wants to Think About Disaster

This past decade has been torn by many disastrous events caused by those who wanted to harm the USA and by natural events such as tornadoes, hurricanes, forest fires, and accidental industrial happenings like oil spills and toxic pollution from transportation accidents. So many things can happen and it is difficult to foresee and to prepare for every event that might occur. If you live in an area that is subject to any of these events, you must consider including your pets in your family plan for disaster preparedness.

This topic must be adapted to your locale, your particular family composition, and certainly to the type and number of pets you have. I strongly recommend you contact your local disaster authorities to see what plans are in place and how they affect you personally. Be sure to ask how pets are covered in the plans, especially in evacuation instructions. Then do your own planning accordingly.

Remember, you must take care of yourself so you can be there to take care of your family, including your dear pets. Certain websites have emergency supply and travel kit lists. These lists are good as the basis for planning, and you can add specific items for your family/pets.

For day to day emergency situations such as an untimely auto accident or being stricken with an illness rendering you unable to communicate, you should display a Rescue Alert Sticker on an entry door outside your home.

It is equally important to carry a wallet emergency card informing first responders and/or medical staff that you have pets in your home that must be cared for in your absence. Both of these items are often available through your local Humane Society or various rescue sites online.

My publisher and I felt this was such an important item, a combination bookmark/emergency wallet card was designed as a gift to those interested in the book.

Here is a copy of the card for your use if you did not receive one with your copy of the book. One side is to identify you as the owner, and the other side gives information on your pets and how to get to them.

NOTICE: I HAVE PETS AT HOME!

My name_____

Address_____

_____

Phone _____

PLEASE HELP! PET INFO ON BACK!

NOTICE: I HAVE PETS AT HOME!

_____-_____

_____-_____

_____-_____

Pet name(s)   Cat/dog/other

Key Keeper:_____phone_____

Vet:_____Phone_____

Perpetual Care

This section of the book offers guidelines for how to ensure that your pet is properly cared for in the event that you become physically unable to do so. The idea that we may leave this earth before our pet(s) is most unsettling—so much so that some humans may repress or ignore these thoughts. But some choose to acknowledge that oftentimes life is unpredictable. We strive to do all we can to express our undying love for our pets, and many find peace in doing their best to plan for the future so that their wishes can be easily followed in their absence.

There are many ways to accomplish this goal of caring for our pets. It may require a combination of methods to ensure your wishes can be followed. Below is a list of suggestions for your review, and the stories that follow demonstrate the importance of completing a plan that includes all your wishes.

Here are some basic thoughts you need to begin the process:

- Age of pet and expected life span for the breed
- Age of owner (your age and the age of the prospective new owner)
- Financial needs of pet—routine annual veterinary care, additional potential health needs, food (special dietary needs), grooming costs, and fencing needs at the new owner's home

The following are just a few major considerations you need to start thinking about as you refine your specific plan:

- Placement with a trusted friend
- Placement with a family member
- Rescue groups—how to select the right one
- Breeders who will take pet back anytime in pet's lifetime
- What you need to get in writing
- List references on will/trust options
- Be specific regarding all details on the final placement of your pet
- Don't neglect to verify the willingness of your choice of person or organization to take on this responsibility before you finalize the plan

This is not an easy task by any stretch of the imagination, but it is one that will make you sleep better after you get it all done. An excellent resource to assist you with this process is a book entitled *Who Will Care When You're Not There?* by Robert E. Kass, JD, LLM & Elizabeth A Carrie, JD, LLM. It is an outstanding legal reference to begin this thought process. The two attorneys who authored this book are undoubtedly animal lovers as well as caring, knowledgeable resources to help you through the planning process. Once this task is done, your own attorney can add any important overlooked details to your estate plan.

If you think you need a lot of money to plan for your pet's future, please rethink that train of thought immediately. As with many things in life, money is not always the answer to every question. What's most important is that you leave detailed directions regarding who will care for your beloved pet companion upon your passing. Do not allow your pet to be sent to a shelter because no one knew what to do. If the thought of this makes your heart ache, then get busy today and get a pet plan in writing.

A Family Story

My only sibling is eight and a half years younger than I am and was a source of much aggravation growing up. Don't get me wrong, I was thrilled when he was born. I was an only child and the thought of having a sibling was exciting. That lasted for a couple of years until he developed a personality all his own. This was one tough little kid—a boisterous boy who was a real challenge as a preschooler. But he was ours and we had to keep him. As ornery as he was, he always adored animals and was kinder to them than he was to me. So there was never a reason to do anything but love him for who he was.

He has been a grown-up for a long time now and has had a lot of life experiences...some good, some not so good. He has a degree in agriculture and works as an owner/consultant.

This businessman who looks like Larry the Cable Guy and dresses like Larry's grandpa is unique. His conversational style is more like Jeff Foxworthy's than that of a corporate type. He leans so far right in his thinking that we all fear he may tip over at any moment. But this hard line conservative is the biggest soft-hearted dog guy you will ever meet.

When he heard about this book and this particular section on how to prepare for your pet in case they survive past your due date, he melted into a pile of marshmallow. His voice quivered as he told me that the one reason he would not get another dog is that he could not bear the thought of someone else trying to take care of his pet. Yet at the same time, he told me that he never wanted to be without a pet.

He attempted to solve his pet attachment problem by finding a breeder who needs a good pet home for one of his stud dogs. This is the perfect solution because the dog will be well cared for and, should he need to place the dog, the breeder will be right there to make sure the dog is cared for properly.

I share this personal story because I know that deep feeling of wanting my companion animals cared for. So whoever you are and whatever you do, stand by your convictions and your dedication to your pet. Find the solution that assures you that all will be OK if something should happen to you. Then make your plan, get it down on paper, and make sure the people who are going to take care of things know your wishes and agree to implement them.

Nina's Story

Nina is an animal lover. She is also a bright and compassionate person whose intelligence forces her to seek information in a highly cognitive way on topics that interest her. One of the most cherished interests she chose to pursue was that of Greece and Greek culture. When she found an opportunity to learn Greek dancing from a Greek native living in her community, she jumped at the chance. She and the instructor found they had many other common interests including cats and a love of the written word. So Nina and her friend shared cat stories and eventually worked together to publish a cookbook.

The friendship that grew during the next few years leads to a story of true dedication that is a pressing example of why to prepare for the care of your pets should you not outlive them. You see, Nina's friend was stricken with a rare and devastating form of dementia several years into their friendship. Since her friend's family lived abroad they could not care for their far-removed family member. It was Nina who stepped forward after it became evident that her friend needed help and support. Nina sought the help of an attorney and remained absent from the meetings as her friend and the attorney took care of the legal matters.

After three years of painful progression of the dementia, Nina's friend passed away. As with any loss of close friends, Nina grieved for her friend but knew she had done her very best. However, she wondered what would happen to the cats. Yes, the friend's cats had been a central part of her life in those years of decline and Nina knew they were very important to her friend. Nina was soon approached by the attorney who had taken care of the legal documents several years before, and to her surprise, her friend had left her the house and the cats plus a handsome stipend to maintain the house until the cats passed on.

You might think the story could end here with a bottom line of, "Wasn't that a wonderful surprise? My friend left me a house and all the cats and some funds to care for them." However, Nina already had a home of her own and worked a full-time job, plus she had her own beloved cats. In one fell swoop she inherited another person's home and all of its contents, which included years of collectibles as well as the resident cats! This might sound like a well-executed plan until one realizes that Nina had to double her daily animal care activities. She had suddenly taken on a tremendous responsibility not really well-detailed in a legal document, and had little idea of how to manage two houses and two families of cats who were not able to be commingled due to personality differences.

Nina's story is still unfolding as this book is being written and was yet another inspiration that moved this book project into reality. There is an obvious need to glean what we can from these experiences.

So my dear friends, the planning guidelines detailed at the beginning of this section come from the experts who have lived by trial and error and have developed their own plans with the knowledge only experience can afford.

Susan's Story

Susan was my dearest friend from grade school. Our lives took very different paths, but we admired each other for our individual choices and shared a deep, unconditional love of our companion animals. Neither of us had human children, but we always had our companion children.

We kept in touch throughout our lives—more so in the later decades—only to find that we got more intense in our love for our pets as we aged. We both had multiple pets at any given time and always put them first on our daily list of priorities. Losing my dearest friend in 2011 was one more driving force to get me started on this book.

Susan's example of thinking and planning ahead for the "unthinkable" shows the careful thought process that is required for the final plan of action. As painful as this is to write, I know in my heart Susan would want everyone who reads this to benefit from any ideas and encouragement they find in her story. She and I discussed this very topic at length, so the outcome of this story is even more painful and heartbreaking to me personally.

After the death of her husband, Susan's health continued to deteriorate, causing her to think about the ultimate fate of her pet companion family. Her pet "children" included many mature pets with health issues of their own. They included a twelve-year-old terrier with control issues, a ten-year-old small breed dog with diabetes, a five-year-old female dog who had just had back surgery and was in a long slow recovery period, two cats who were nine and ten years old, and two younger cats from a shelter that were one and two years old. In addition she had three birds whose ages are not readily recalled, but I do know she had them for several years and none were young at the time she adopted them.

I cannot imagine how she felt the night she summoned the ambulance as she was experiencing her fatal heart attack. Fortunately she had enlisted the help of a friend to come to her home and care for the pets should she become ill or be taken to the hospital, and her dear friend did just that.

When Susan's niece called to share the sad news of her aunt's death, I asked about the pets and she assured me that they were taken by this wonderful friend and that Susan had detailed in her will how they should ultimately be cared for. Several months later I learned that indeed my friend did have a detailed will, but no trust document to implement her very detailed wishes! Her niece was contacted by another attorney and told that the will she was trying to execute had not been properly filed.

Without belaboring the point that each of us must take care of our estate planning, I cannot stress enough how important it is to finish your plans and sign off on them with your attorney. What could have been an excellent example of a happy ending for my friend's beloved family and the pet companions she cherished has now turned into a nightmare.

Susan's niece has been denied the option to retain family heirlooms, which she loved and hoped to give to her children. The shelter that had placed the two young cats has accepted them back for re-homing. The birds have been placed with friends and are doing well. However, the dear friend who has the three older and infirm dogs and the older cats has not received any monetary assistance with their medical costs. I am confident that Susan had considered these needs in her well-thought-out plan. This has created a financial burden for this friend. The friend now finds herself in the age-old predicament of "no good deed goes unpunished."

The grown stepchildren who had never really known Susan are executing an old will that did not include Susan's carefully planned wishes for her pets. These heirs have no real firsthand knowledge of her wishes and, as often happens in cases like this, have no legal obligation to respect her final wishes contained in a will that was not filed properly.

The lessons that can be drawn from this story are many—most importantly to get the right document drawn up, signed, and legally enforceable upon your death. If you do not spell it out and have it done in the proper way, your wishes simply will not be followed.

The specific lesson here is if you truly love your pets, do what is necessary to make sure they will be taken care of; think through the plan you want implemented and then get busy and DO IT! The pets cannot speak for themselves and my heart breaks for the family and friends who are struggling with the circumstances in the story above.

GRIEVING THE LOSS OF
OUR BELOVED COMPANION ANIMALS

Evidence of the domestication of dogs can be seen in cave drawings made between 14,000 and 30,000 B.C. The domestication of cats came later at about 8,500 B.C. It seems reasonable to assume that when these companions died, the human emotion that resulted could be termed grief.

In ancient Egypt, pet owners shaved their eyebrows and smeared mud in their hair during the mourning period after the loss of a pet dog. This grieving ritual lasted several days and included mourning aloud. I find current cultural ways to mourn just as effective, and the one thing I know for sure is that it is not healthy for any of us not to mourn.

Certainly each of us needs to find our best way to grieve. No matter who you are, no matter what your position in life or your perceived "need" to keep a stiff upper lip, showing your emotions at the loss of a beloved pet is just a healthy and OK thing to do. So all you tough guys can loosen up. There are many ways we can mourn and hopefully you can find a way that suits your heart best.

I have included some thoughts on personal grieving and ways you can help your family and friends through this difficult time. My own personal stories will hopefully serve as examples of how to deal with this difficult time and will inspire you to invent new ways to bring yourself to a place of closure. You will never forget your companions—they are forever in your heart. Pad the loss with all those wonderful memories of the good times.

After your loss, your veterinarian can often help with burial or cremation options. Be sure to listen carefully to your vet and not take things the wrong way. When you are grieving, it's easy to misconstrue heartfelt and sincere well-meaning advice. I had no idea how I felt about cremation until I lost my first pet as an adult. My father had always buried our pets in our yard and we knew they were there and had fond memories of our time on earth together. But as an adult I was living in a suburban area where yard space was an issue. Also, losing a pet in the dead of winter with hard frozen ground presented another obstacle. The choice of many urban or suburban dwellers is cremation, but I just could not get used to the idea that my beloved pet would have no gravesite. So at the suggestion of a friend, we utilized a lovely pet cemetery in the area which offered us the in-ground burial to which we were accustomed. This ritual of burying our pets has brought us to a place of closure and was an integral part of the grieving process. This may not be for everyone but it is definitely an option to consider. I visit Memory Park Pet Cemetery annually, where the peace and tranquility of the setting calms my soul.

There are as many options for our pets as there are for humans, and you should do whatever you feel best reflects your feelings for your beloved pet. We have many cultural and religious rituals that define who we are and we should definitely do whatever makes us feel like we have done our best.

An excellent resource for suggestions on loss and grieving our pets can be found on the Internet under the topic "Veterinary Medicine" and the subtopic "Loss and Grief." Sites offer many resources including a pet loss support hotline. Other topics covered include the gut-wrenching question of "How to know when it is time to say goodbye," hospice care for pets, pet memorials, and pet care planning if they happen to outlive us.

Remember, we all grieve in our own way. Never feel this is a sign of weakness. On the contrary, it is normal to mourn and there are many ways to grieve. I feel for those who do not understand the deep feelings of loss associated with losing a companion animal. But you have to take care of your own needs without regard for those who simply do not comprehend your loss. You can always help these poor folks later—at this time you need to take care of yourself and those close to you, including other pets in the family.

Many times the remaining pets mourn the loss of their friend. Be mindful of their needs too since they often help by consoling you. My remaining pets were such a source of strength after my losses. I wouldn't have coped nearly as well without them. I would recommend spending more time with them—either just sitting quietly and petting them or taking them for a long walk or a romp in the park. We must bear in mind that they too are experiencing the loss of a companion.

Many people think that the best way to alleviate their grief over the loss of a pet is to rush out and get another one. Please consider this very carefully, then DO NOT DO ANYTHING for at least a week or longer. This caveat applies to both you and to anyone who might try to cheer up their friends or family during a time of grief. Most companion animals are considered part of the family and they simply cannot be replaced. What we hope to accomplish by rushing out and adopting another pet is to fill the space they have left in our aching hearts. During those first few days and weeks it is best to let the heart heal by doing the things that comfort you. Then, using the guides found in the preceding chapters, you can start the process of choosing a new pet in a calm and realistic state of mind. At the end of this section there is a story relating just how important it is to consider the feelings of the remaining pets. Please read "The Meeting" at the end of the chapter "Communicating Our Sorrow" and you will see what I mean.

In the past I have found it extremely beneficial to the grieving process for me to publish tributes in memory of my pets in either breed club journals or online forums. I have included some of these stories from my heart on the next pages. I feel they speak for themselves when it comes to expressing the feelings I am sure many of you have felt or possibly will feel someday about a pet.

The hurt of each loss is something I will remember forever, but as with all traumas in life we must learn to cope, recover, and move forward. To help myself move forward I employed a technique endorsed by newspaper advice columnist Ann Landers for evaluating our important life relationships—I made a list of the pros and cons of having pets in my life. The pros so outnumbered the cons of having to endure the sadness of their loss that I am now living with numbers fourteen and fifteen.

I am not a glutton for punishment. I just realize that I would never want to forfeit the wonderful times I have with my pets on a daily basis just because I may lose them someday. I treasure each moment with them and consider them a blessing beyond description.

COMMUNICATING OUR SORROW

Below are a few examples of how simply writing a letter can help you or your friends with the grieving process. As I stated in many ways throughout this book, my companion animals have brought me in contact with so many wonderful people. Some have become friends, others just passed through my life, and some have no idea how much I admire them and their dedication to their pets or to various rescue activities. The following email is a classic example—it is from a family I have never met who took the time to do so much and then express their deepest feelings of grief and gratitude when they lost their precious dog Molly.

This email was forwarded to me by my dear friend Janice, who has tirelessly worked full-time for twenty-five years as a coordinator for Spotsavers, a St. Louis-based Dalmatian rescue that helped place Molly. Janice is the supreme conduit of all things good and kind. The Stoverink family also demonstrates goodness and kindness. It is not surprising that they shared a very special way to help the spirit heal at a time of great loss, and I am glad that Janice shared this letter with all of us. Letting others know how much Molly meant says so much to my heart—I share it now to speak to you.

Hi there,

I am not sure if you remember us or not, but my name is Trish Stoverink and my family adopted Holly from Spotsavers about eleven years ago. Holly was found abandoned and pregnant in Potosi, Missouri eleven years ago around Christmastide. It turned out that she had six puppies—then two of them died, but with a strange turn of events she ended up taking care of thirteen puppies needing mothering! I believe Holly and her puppies were fostered by a woman named Susan. Anyway, my fourth grade class ended up raising money for Holly and her puppies. My family ended up adopting her and changed her name to Molly.

Unfortunately, on Easter Sunday she passed away after about two months of intense pain due to a tumor that started in her brain and spread throughout her body. We tried everything we could but lost her on Sunday after several intensive seizures.

She was an extremely important member of our family and we are devastated to lose her. We never had a dog that became such a vital part of our family before. Molly was the highlight of all of our lives. I actually moved out close to two years ago to attend Webster University, but I had to make it home at least once a week to see her.

She was the center of our lives for eleven years and I don't know what we are going to do without her. I just wanted to let you know about our loss since Spotsavers was so influential in bringing her into our lives. You cannot imagine the joy she brought us. I attached a few pictures so you can see just how loved she was. You gave us a member of our family and for that we are extremely thankful.

Sincerely,
The Stoverink Family

Here is a letter I wrote to a friend and her husband on the loss of their beloved cat. This letter hopefully let them know I understood the feelings she and her husband were experiencing right then.

Dear Sharon and Mike,

It has been a trying three weeks for us all with your loss and my health emergency with my husband. The night you called to tell me that Bentley was not responding as you had hoped to the fluids and that it might be time to let him rest, I was reminded of all the times I was at that place myself. We talked a bit and you verbally reviewed all the pieces of the decision making puzzle you knew you had to complete. Your veterinarian was cooperating with the care plan you all had chosen but was getting sort of blasé when you asked for his evaluation. Since he knows you are such committed animal lovers, I suppose one could think he was being non-committal.

However, I hope you know that when you talked to me I truly wanted to know all your thoughts—no matter what they were and no matter how many times or ways you had to say them. Right then you just needed a friend who understood your sorrow.

In fact, at that moment I did not need to even remember that you and Mike and Bentley found one another when you were not looking for a stray cat. What I did remember was that you all joined paws (including your canine girls) and became a family that lived and loved together.

Bentley loved his new home and his family and he was such a social boy. He didn't care that you are mature, accomplished humans in your own fields and I know he couldn't have cared less the night you were entertaining nationally renowned educational experts. Not my lovely friend Bentley—he just loved being with us all and getting a pet and moving among us to rub his scent on our legs or our arms. He was a gentle and calming soul, and I will always remember him that way.

I know how hard it was to see him decline. You gave much thought and effort to helping him regain his health, but it was just his time. I am so sorry your community veterinarian let you down at this most emotional time. His "casual" remarks when you took Bentley to him for the last time were unforgivable.

Your mixed feelings toward your veterinarian at this emotional time are justified (especially when you received a rather casual and insincere note some weeks later along with the bill for the last visit). When you needed consoling at the time of Bentley's death, the veterinarian just did what needed to be done in a clinical and perfunctory way, then several weeks later sent a bill and no real mention of your loss. Our mixed feelings toward your veterinarian at this emotional time (especially when you received a rather casual and insincere note some weeks later along with the bill for the last visit) are justified. When you needed consoling at the time of Bentley's death the veterinarian just did what needed to be done in a clinical and perfunctory way. Then several weeks later sent a bill and no real mention of your loss.

When a vet gets to the point where he or she feels their job is so routine that they do not see or feel the bond you have with your pet or relate to your loss, it may be time to find a different veterinarian.

This was your Bentley—you loved him, you cared for him, he loved you back. He was Mike's little boy one day and his buddy the next. He was always there, sharing your space, your life, and his very essence of feline-ery with you.

At that moment of grief you needed a friend—a friend who has experienced the same kind of emotional loss. You needed an understanding ear and assurance that you had done your very best for Bentley. That was the least and the most I could do at that fragile time.

He will be in your heart forever. You know that his life and yours intertwined for a reason. You shall always have a bank of fond Bentley memories and you will cherish those thoughts of him always.

With all my heart and pet-mom feelings,
Barbara

The Meeting—An Example of Sympathy Gone Awry

Early in our canine parenthood we could not conceive of the emotional pain of losing one of our canines. No one really wants to think about the sad parts of life. But our first-born canine, Chrissy the Boxer, crossed the Rainbow Bridge after a bout with seizures and liver disease at age eleven. This loss affected us all, including Chrissy's faithful companion Red Barron, a scholarly and well-behaved red Doberman. Barron showed all the classic signs of mourning. He had loss of appetite and spent the days quietly resting alone in the bedroom. Then a well-meaning friend changed everything!

One day the doorbell rang and my husband insisted I answer the bell. I would soon learn it was a "set up." When I opened the door, a dear friend was there holding a thin cord attached to what appeared to be sixty-five pounds of black and tan muscle in a state of sheer excitement. My initial feeling of surprise was followed by a slew of raw emotions. How could anyone bring me another dog? Chrissy could never be replaced. We needed more time. Poor Barron would be confused.

Well, what happened next will give every behaviorist and every mature adult good reason to reprimand. The timing of the introduction was bad, the place was bad, and the surprise was painful. Our not yet new and wonderful "daughter" Doberman lunged into the entry hall, Barron came to see what was happening, and in an instant the "new daughter" had nipped his nose!

This five second canine soap opera scene could have been prevented with proper planning, but my first impulse at this point was to keep these two angry Dobermans apart. So I took Barron by the collar, brought him into the bedroom, and shut the door. I sat on the bed and cried.

The next two weeks were indescribable. Josephine now had a name. She had come from a shelter and needed to be spayed, so that was done. In my mind this was a necessity and would make it easier for us to find her a home since she and Barron could not be in the same room together, or so we thought.

Then one fateful Saturday our friend came by as he had done several times since delivering Josephine. We all agreed that the hasty move to get another companion for Barron just was not working. We would all work to find Josephine a forever home. At this point Barron was resting in the bedroom and Josie was outside. Barron very quietly came down the hallway toward the kitchen. The humans were all talking so we did not hear him. My husband opened the back door leading to the dog run and in bounced Josephine. Horror struck me. We were about to witness a face-off. Barron moved behind me and started a low growl with the hair on his back slowly bristling. I had never seen him like this before. My husband grabbed Josephine, who was desperately trying to get loose. I was ready for the worst and called to our friend, "Be ready to grab Josie." He nodded and in a split second she ran the few feet in front of Barron and rolled on her back in a completely vulnerable position. Barron sauntered over, sniffed the obligatory canine sniff, and walked slowly into the bedroom for a nap.

Three humans (apparently uneducated in canine behavior) stood there totally stunned and relieved. How ridiculous. We had not let these wonderfully smart and sweet canines engage in the ritual of canine acquaintanceship. To this day we chuckle over it, but we realize that we could have handled this introduction in a much more sensible way. Thank the guardian angel of the canines that she was with us that day.

Red Barron and Josephine became inseparable until his journey to the Rainbow Bridge some six years later. They played together, slept by one another, and shared many afternoons in their play yard. When Josie lost Barron she visibly mourned, curling up on the bed for days. When we introduced her to her new companion, we did so on neutral ground (in this case the driveway) where neither could stake a claim. We of course had them both on a leash and made sure not to do anything to overwhelm Josie. They met and sniffed each other, which is the canine introductory rite of making sure this is someone they like. I am happy to report we had learned our lesson and this time all went swimmingly. The new team of Josephine and Sparky the Dalmatian was born and the Levy canine crew carried on the tradition of love and companionship.

These are the lessons:

- Bringing someone a gift of another dog is just not a good idea. It does not always turn out to be fine and could even spell disaster to the pet relationship or the end of a human friendship if you don't consider their feelings and their ability to cope with and care for a new pet.

- Always let new canines meet in a controlled and neutral environment, then extend that supervision to other territory in the house or yard, possessions such as toys, and most importantly food/treats. Canines do not always understand "sharing," so supervised training is needed.

Saving a pet from a shelter is a great idea and this "save" turned out to be wonderful, since Josephine was indeed a smart, loyal little girl with an excellent temperament. Considering the difficulty shelters have with placing large black dogs, Josephine was a find we did not want to miss.

Now we know—we could have made life so much easier for ourselves if our friend had found Josephine and then given us a gift certificate for this special little girl (gift certificates are available at almost every shelter or rescue group). Then we could have met her and arranged for her to meet Red Barron while the shelter folks were there to help and give us tips on her temperament.

There is no doubt we would have fallen in love with this delightful girl who kissed everyone and loved life to the hilt. I offer you the benefit of our learning experience to make your pet selection process a whole lot more pleasant and joyful. Remember they love you more than you can even imagine.

SHARING YOUR COMPASSION

As a friend you can:

- Make a scrapbook page with a picture of the pet in happier times.
- Send a handwritten note or letter to your friends with at least one happy memory of their pet in the text.
- Send a sympathy card with or without a short personal message along with your heartfelt sympathy.
- Send a tribute in memory of the pet to a rescue or shelter organization you know is important to your friend.
- Send a book about losing a pet—there are many lovely books written on this subject available at local bookstores or online. Some of these books are written especially for children who may be experiencing the loss of a pet for the first time.
- Call your friend and share stories about the pet. Always let them know you understand their loss and assure them they did all they could to help the pet.
- Let them know about grieving programs—you could do a search and offer the search results to them.
- If you can afford to do so, one of the most rewarding ways I have found to let a friend know that I truly share in their sadness is to send a tribute to a pet-associated health foundation that relates to the lost pet's illness.

There are many ways to show your compassion at times of loss. Remember, no matter how small the gesture on your part, I can assure you it will be appreciated.

Tributes to Your Pet

As I mentioned before, writing tributes to be published in breed newsletters or online is a wonderful way to pay tribute to your beloved companion animals. Below are two of the many tributes I struggled to write but found so rewarding when I read them in print. It does not matter if the writing is perfect. The feelings we express on paper can sometimes give the release we need to deal with our grief. If you think this may help you, please go ahead. You need not impress anyone—this is for you and your pet.

**KAY KAY LEVY
(COBBLESTONE YENTA)
1994 - 2006**

From the moment we knew you existed, you became our Kay Kay. Your dad flew to Virginia to get you and fly you back in the cabin with him. When I arrived at the airport he was carrying you in your flight bag and I ran to meet you. As soon as we unzipped the bag, out flew that "famous face" and—zap—the kiss that bonded us forever!

You were the cutest Black & Tan puppy! Your shining eyes saw it all and your famous "wild woman" personality had the four geriatric

Cavaliers you were destined to rejuvenate rolling their eyes when you bounded into a room.

In addition to teething on every piece of furniture we owned and destroying the kitchen wall (none of which was your fault according to your daddy), you brought us love, energy, and the sheer will of those double digit Cavaliers to live through your puppy year and into adolescence.

At seven years old, you overcame a near-fatal illness that left me praying for just one more day. We were blessed with four more years of your "sassiness," and you made the loss of all four of your elderly siblings easier to bear. You were the thread of hope through personal illness.

You became the "leader" for your younger siblings, but never gave up the title of "Mom's favorite Black & Tan earthling baby." You coined the phrase "geriatric puppy."

Your last battle was swift. The loss is still surreal to me at times, although the sorrow is still fresh in my mind and painful to my heart. We will never forget you—you are still with us in many ways and will always remain a part of our hearts and thoughts.

You are now pain-free and can once again enjoy romping with those geriatric Cavaliers you called your siblings. You got Dad and I settled into our Cavalier Cottage and a quieter lifestyle. We had so hoped you could stay a while longer, but we suppose you felt your job was done here on earth.

We will all be together again someday—if I did not believe that, my love, I simply could not go on with life.

Watch over us, Daddy's Angel, until we meet again.

Your adoring family,
Ken, Barbara, Winnie, Francie, and Mikey

WINNIE LEVY
1996-2010

The call finally came. Lucky Star Cavalier Rescue had managed to buy nine wonderful Cavaliers at auction who were now ready to leave that awful world of a puppy mill and find well-deserved forever homes. I checked online to read their vital statistics. My name had come up as a potential adoptee. We chose the oldest— the one who needed the knee surgery. I was afraid no one else would want her, and something just said to me, "This is your little girl and you can call her Winnie after your mom." At that moment this precious Blenheim baby girl was mine—part of my heart.

The rescue representative called to arrange the pick-up. She had some obscure registry papers but she did have lineage. Did I recognize any of these names? About four names into the list I gasped—a familiar kennel name and an even more familiar registered name. She was the great-granddaughter of our April!

April was a re-home from a breeder who had already bred the five litters allowed by the registry at that time. She was afraid of storms and very shy, so unless I wanted her she would have been put down. Well, she came to us and lived another ten years! She ruled from the center pillow of our king-sized bed, perched on a pillow sham.

Winnie came to us on December 11, 1999. She became my mother's namesake, was in good general health, and had a tail velocity of 100 miles per hour. She slept for years on the center pillow sham on the king-sized bed as if she had always known that was where she belonged. She had the sweetest little face and eyes in the world, and snored all the way home that fateful day she came to be ours.

Although Winnie developed heart valve disease, she did quite well until three years ago. But each health problem was overcome by our determined girl and each recovery seemed to make her stronger. But finally her number was called—she sank to the floor and I picked her up and put her on a soft pad. As I held her close on the way to the hospital, she quietly began her ascent to the Rainbow Bridge. As the emergency team opened the car door I knew she had gone on to wait for me—to go be with Mikey, who had gone only three weeks before.

Miss Winnie was meant to be ours, and as she aged she took on the role of headmistress of the Cavalier Cottage, which suited her younger brother Mikey just fine. Losing her has left such sadness in our lives and hearts. Her small headstone reads my heartfelt words—Always and Forever~Mommy's Baby Girl.

Winnie is survived by her mom and dad, Barbara and Ken Levy, and a host of dedicated veterinarians at the University of Missouri College of

Veterinary Medicine. For several years this brilliant and compassionate team put the quality of Winnie's life first and in turn gave her longevity with the dignity she deserved. Up until she left us for the Rainbow Bridge, she barked at the squirrels on the fence outside her porch…because she felt up to it. Our thanks and blessings to all of her veterinarians.

Strengthening Our Memories

Well dear pet parents, no matter the origin of your precious one, they are a part of your life now. If you have not begun to save or organize all those great pictures and memorabilia, now is the time. You have chronicled their "story" in your mind. You know it by heart and tell it often, but now is the time to write it down for posterity. Don't worry if the writing is not perfect or if it is even typed—just do it. You will feel so warm and fuzzy once it's done, and have a great time reminiscing and reliving those wonderful moments. Start a life journal or binder, even if they were not a baby when they came to you. It can be their adoption story, their "the day I saw you at the shelter" story, or "the day I visited the breeder and there you were" story. The important thing is to get it down on paper or store it electronically with lots of pictures to memorialize your time together.

Ways to do this include some very inexpensive ways to begin:

- Loose leaf binder with three hole punched paper (great for children to draw and paste photos)
- Traditional scrapbooking
- Electronic scrapbook/document organizing
- Puppy baby books (purchased online and in specialty pet stores)

Any method is fine, and it will feel great to immortalize your pet and record what a special place they hold in your life. Just to get you going, here are examples from my very own scrapbook and some pages from friends and family who wanted to share the love they have for the pets that will be forever in their hearts.

Following are samples from scrapbooks:

Strengthening Our Memories

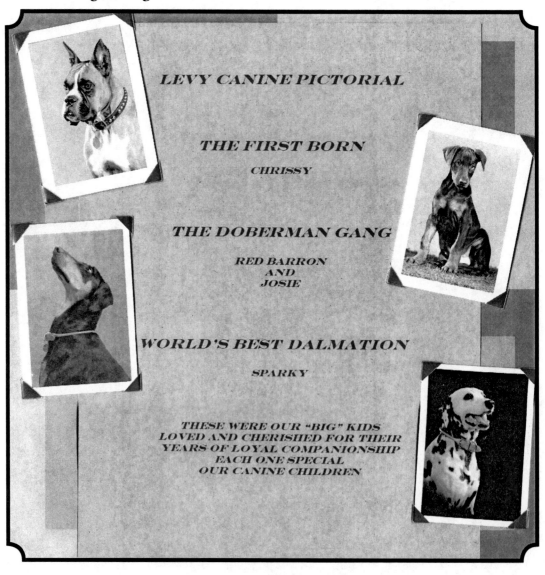

LEVY CANINE PICTORIAL

THE FIRST BORN

CHRISSY

THE DOBERMAN GANG

RED BARRON
AND
JOSIE

WORLD'S BEST DALMATION

SPARKY

THESE WERE OUR "BIG" KIDS
LOVED AND CHERISHED FOR THEIR
YEARS OF LOYAL COMPANIONSHIP
EACH ONE SPECIAL
OUR CANINE CHILDREN

Strengthening Our Memories

Mikey Jimi and his namesake who is also his Godfather-the one who saved his life.

Strengthening Our Memories

Magenta

Twitch

"Tge Girls"...
on maneuvers!

Strengthening Our Memories

"Monet"
1994-2012

FINAL THOUGHTS FROM THE AUTHOR

It seems we have come to a point where we have examined a comprehensive list of topics covering companion animals in general, our relationships with them, and most importantly, our responsibility to them. Hopefully we have navigated all the major phases of pet companion ownership, including:

- thinking about owning a pet
- researching all the ways to find "our" pet companion
- making sure we choose the best pet
- considering all costs—both the emotional and the financial costs
- taking proper care of our pet
- planning for the pet if they should out live us
- and finally, grieving the loss of our pet.

This book has been a labor of love and a wonderful opportunity to share a lifetime (at least up to now) of experiences.

If the reader gets one answer or one helpful thought for a happier life with their pet, then my job is done here. It is my hope that you discover many positive insights.

The quest of enjoying life can and does take on many forms. Age has taught me that experiences can indeed help us make better decisions. Our life experiences can help us make better decisions about what to do, and sometimes, more importantly, what not to do.

When it is the right time and you are enjoying life with the "right" pet companion, it just does not get any better. Now go and "kiss" your buddy or your baby and play like you feel on top of the world.

RELATED SUGGESTED READING

The Health Benefits of Dog Walking for Pets and People: Evidence and Case Studies (New Directions in the Human-Animal Bond Series) Rebecca A. Johnson, Alan M. Beck and Sandra McCune, editors.
Purdue University Press 2011

Walk a Hound, Lose a Pound: How You and Your Dog Can Lose Weight, Stay Fit, and Have Fun Together (New Directions in the Human-Animal Bond Series); Phil Zeltzman and Rebecca A. Johnson, authors. Purdue University Press 2011

Once a Stray; Joanie Fedyk. (This book is a guide to understanding the value and enjoyment of therapy dogs.) Dog Ear Publishing 2011

Who Will Care When You're Not There? Estate Planning for Pet Owners; Robert E. Kass, JD, LLM and Elizabeth A. Carrie, JD, LLM. Carob Tree Press 2011

Companion Animals: Their Biology, Care, Health, and Management Karen L. Campbell and John R. Campbell. Pearson Prentice Hall 2005, 2009

ACKNOWLEDGEMENTS

As this book took on a life of its own, I found myself looking to my pool of veterinary professionals, who helped me confirm research facts when there were inconsistencies or opposing views. Internet research is great, but it takes a solid knowledge base and lots of experience to tell the facts from the myths and misinformation. I am in awe of their expertise and humbled by their willingness to help a novice writer.

Here is the composition of the voluntary editorial board that gave so generously of their time and knowledge. It was a gift to me and I share it all with you, the readers, who will also benefit from their knowledge and kindness.

F.A. (Tony) Mann, DVM, MS, Diplomate ACVECC, Professor, Small Animal Soft Tissue Surgeon, Director of Small Animal Emergency and Critical Care Services, University of Missouri Veterinary Medical Teaching Hospital

Jeffrey R. Coggan DVM, Practitioner and Partner, Clark Animal Hospital 10510 Manchester Road, St. Louis, MO, Member Hospital-AAHA

John R. Dodam, DVM, MS, PhD, Chair, Department of Veterinary Medicine and Surgery, University of Missouri College of Veterinary Medicine

Leah A. Cohn, DVM, PhD, Diplomate, ACVIM (SAIM), Professor, Veterinary Medicine, Dept. Veterinary Medicine and Surgery, University of Missouri-College of Veterinary Medicine

Rebecca A. Johnson, PhD, RN, FAAN, FNAP, President, International Association of Human-Animal Interaction Organizations (IAHAIO), Professor and Director, Research Center for Human-Animal Interaction (ReCHAI), College of Veterinary Medicine, Millsap Professor of Gerontological Nursing, Sinclair School of Nursing, University of Missouri

Tim J. Evans, DVM, MS, PhD, Diplomate ACT and ABVT, Technology Section Leader, Medical Diagnostic Laboratory, Associate Professor, Department of Veterinary Pathobiology, University of Missouri College of Veterinary Medicine

Mary Molly Murphy Flanders, RVT, VTS (EEC), First certified emergency and critical care specialist at University of Missouri Veterinary Medical Teaching Hospital, 2005 Chancellor's Outstanding Staff Award, Lectured at multiple veterinary conferences in the US and at University College in Dublin, Ireland

All these thoughtful people practice their chosen profession with the knowledge and compassion it takes to be so good at what they do. Somehow they keep their constant focus on delivery of the best pet care while educating new generations of veterinarians and human-animal bond professionals. They share their knowledge in a comparative medicine environment, which benefits humans as well as companion animals. My sincere appreciation to each and every one of them for helping me achieve my dream.

SHARING WITH AND FOR OUR PETS

To enhance the lives of pets, the author plans to share a portion of the profits from this book to support those who care for our pets, including the following rescue groups and veterinary teaching projects:

Jodie's Eyes Comparative Ophthalmology Development Fund—This veterinary ophthalmology service fund is used for patient care, service members' research, and development/educational activities for ophthalmology staff. It offers assistance to those researching eye problems in our pet companion animals. It is administered under the direction of Elizabeth A. Giuliano, DVM, MS, Diplomate ACVO, Associate Professor and Section Leader, Ophthalmology, University of Missouri College of Veterinary Medicine.

Respiratory-Bronchial Tree Model Project—This special project is a joint venture between an engineer and the Department of Internal Medicine at University of Missouri College of Veterinary Medicine. Using images obtained from a computed tomographic (CT) scan of a dog, a model of the airways will be created. This windpipe/bronchial tree will be replicated in a flexible model for teaching endoscopic examinations (a highly skilled medical procedure), to residents in training. This will allow trainees to learn how to examine the inside of companion animals' lungs for quicker and safer retrieval of objects obstructing the airway, and to diagnose diseases of the lung requiring expert navigation into the airways. Quicker retrieval of an object or quicker diagnosis of a tumor or disease will greatly improve the treatment and outcome for our pets. This project is directed by Carol Renerio, DVM.

ReCHAI (Research Center for Human-Animal Interaction)—ReCHAI conducts programs and studies that engage people and companion animals in creative ways to benefit those on both ends of the leash. Their work includes studying the health benefits of dog walking and the stress reducing qualities of human–animal interaction in a wide range of people, including U.S. military veterans, older adults, abused children, children with autism, and prison inmates. This internationally recognized program is directed by Dr. Rebecca A. Johnson, PhD, RN, FAAN, FNAP, President, International Association of Human-Animal Interaction Organizations (IAHAIO), Professor and Director of ReCHAI, College of Veterinary Medicine, Millsap Professor of Gerontological Nursing, Sinclair School of Nursing, University of Missouri.

In addition, the author may offer discounts and/or a portion of sales for approved organizations in conjunction with special events and/or book signings. Requests must be submitted in writing detailing the organization's mission statement and purpose. Visit www.CreativeCavalierLLC.com to submit your request.

CPSIA information can be obtained at www.ICGtesting.com
Printed in the USA
LVOW11s0819020913

350496LV00002B/14/P

9 781936 688630